# CLIMATE CHANGE

*To*
*my fellow Columban missionaries for their support and friendship*

Seán McDonagh

# Climate Change
## THE CHALLENGE TO ALL OF US

the columba press

First published in 2006 by
the columba press
55A Spruce Avenue, Stillorgan Industrial Park,
Blackrock, Co Dublin

Cover by Bill Bolger
Origination by The Columba Press
Printed in Ireland by ColourBooks Ltd, Dublin

ISBN 1 85607 562 1

*Acknowledgements*

I would like to thank Elizabeth McArdle for all the help she has given
me while writing this book. Thanks also to Fr Pat Connaughton for
proof-reading it on a number of occasions. Finally, thanks to the editor,
Seán O Boyle for many helpful suggestions.

# Table of Contents

# Introduction

In January 2006, three politicians from different parts of the world acknowledged that the consequences of global warming could be much worse than previously thought. In his address on Australia Day 2006 the Governor-General, Michael Jeffery, warned Australians that, 'one of the most daunting environmental challenges is global warming'.[1] Former President Bill Clinton told the Davos World Economic Forum in Switzerland that climate change was the most pressing threat which we now face. It has the power to end the march of civilisation as we know it.[2] The British Prime Minister, Tony Blair, in a preface in the book entitled *Avoiding Dangerous Climate Change*, wrote that, 'it is clear from the work presented here that the risks of climate change may well be greater than we thought'.[3]

Sir David King, the chief scientific advisor to the UK government, has repeatedly stated that 'the problems arising from global warming are the biggest challenges facing governments'.[4] James Lovelock, the scientist who wrote the very popular book *Gaia: A New Look at Life on Earth* in the late 1970s, has written a new book called *The Revenge of Gaia*. In his new book he predicts that global warming will drive temperatures in the temperate zones up by 8 degrees celsius and by 5 degrees celsius in the tropics within the 21st century. Climate change will also disrupt the world's thermohaline system which distributes heat around the world through ocean currents. David Attenborough,

1. Stephanie, Peatling, 'Our golden soil is in danger, Jeffery warns', *The Sydney Morning Herald*, 27 January 2006, www.smh.com.au/news/national

2. 'Clinton's climate change threat', *The Sunday Independent*, 29 January 2006, page 16.

3. Michael McCarthy, 'Climate poses increased threat, admits Blair', *The Independent*, 30 January 2006. www.news.independent.co.uk 30/01/2006 page 1 of 2.

4. Eco Quotes, *The Guardian*, Environment Supplement, 3 November 2004, page 12.

a long-time skeptic of climate change, is now convinced that global warming is happening. As a result, he took part in a two-part BBC documentary on climate change and its consequence in May and June of 2006. His reason for sounding the alarm is very simple. 'How could I look my grandchildren in the eye and say I knew about this and I did nothing'.[5]

Two studies published in the journal *Science* in March 2006 predicted that by 2100 sea levels could rise by 6 metres. Dr Bette Otto-Bliesner, the principal author of one of these studies, used a wide range of data from ancient corals, and ice cores from the Arctic and Antarctic to build up an adequate computer model. When he ran the model backwards he found the results to be accurate. Then he ran the model forward and found that sea levels could rise by 5 or 6 metres over 100 years.[6] The impact of this on ecosystems would be enormous and would create very unpleasant living conditions for millions of humans.[7] Huge areas of Dublin, Cork, Waterford, Belfast and many cities elsewhere, especially in the Majority World would be inundated.

In countries of the South, now often called the Majority World, the situation will be even worse. Christian Aid predicts that in Sub-Saharan Africa alone, by the end of the century, 182 million people could die from diseases which are attributable to global warming.[8] Diseases such as malaria, cholera, dengue

---

5. Stuart Wavell, 'It's serious – Attenborough says stop climate change', *The Sunday Independent*, news review, 21 May 2006 page 8.
6. Dick Ahlstrom, 'Six-metre sea level rise predicted', *The Irish Times*, 24 March 2006, page 15.
7. James Lovelock, *The Revenge of Gaia*, Penguin, London, 2006.
8. It is very difficult to find the right term to describe the relationship between rich and poor countries today. In the 1960s, 1970s and 1980s the terms First World and Third World were used but many people living in Third World countries dislike being placed in the third place. Others use the terms developed and developing. Since it is developed economics which are destroying the earth, encouraging other countries to follow this path is like promoting collective suicide. I find both of these terms unacceptable. Some use the terms North and South since most of the rich countries are in the North. However, Australia and New Zealand are in the South. In recent years, people have begun using the terms Majority and Minority Worlds. This is a simple demographic

fever and Rift Valley fever will become more prevalent and spread to hitherto unaffected places.[9]

Chapter one of the book deals with the atmosphere and attempts to separate out naturally occurring warming and cooling periods of the earth's history from human-induced climate change. Chapter two, entitled 'Climate Change and Extreme Weather' investigates the connection between climate change and extreme weather patterns. Chapter three looks at the impact of climate change on the oceans and the living world. Chapter four surveys the various responses to climate change, ranging from denial to attempts to address it. Chapter five outlines the run-up to the Kyoto Protocol on limiting greenhouse gases in 1997 and what has been achieved since. Some people put forward nuclear power as a way of dealing with climate change. Chapter six investigates that claim. Chapter seven concentrates on what can be done to reduce greenhouse gas emissions by promoting both energy efficiency and renewable sources of energy. Chapter eight discusses what is involved in the concept of 'peak oil' and how that will effect modern transport systems, especially road and air transport. The final chapter looks at how the churches have responded to the challenge of climate change and what the churches should be doing to address this enormous challenge in the next few years.

Unfortunately, the problems associated with global warming, or even the wider environment, did not figure in either Pope Benedict's first encyclical *Deus Caritas Est* or his 2006 address to the diplomatic corps assigned to the Holy See. This is disappointing because the threat to the environment did appear in Pope John Paul II's first encyclical *Redemptor Hominis* which was published in March 1979. He reflected on Saint Paul's statement in the Epistle to the Romans 8:2 that 'creation (that) has been groaning in travail together until now' and applied it to the

mark of identity. Most of the poor people on the planet live in the Majority World. Most of the rich live in the Minority world.
9. John Vidal, 'Africa climate change could kill millions', *The Guardian*, 15 May 2006, page 25.

ecological damage which is happening globally. But even he did not specifically mention global warming. Pope Benedict did speak of the need to protect the environment during his Pentecost homily on Sunday 4 June 2006.

The purpose of this book is to help the reader understand that climate change is not just one environmental problem among a host of others. With the possible exception of the massive extinction of species which is currently under way, climate change is by far the most serious environmental issue facing humankind and the planet. In fact, many would consider it the most serious emergency the human race has every faced.

Bearing that in mind, it should be a top priority for the Catholic Church if the church really believes that its mission is for the flourishing of the life of the world.

Fortunately, global warming is moving towards centre stage in the Anglican Church in Britain. On 28 March 2006, the Archbishop of Canterbury, Dr Rowan Williams, during an interview on BBC Radio 4, told British political leaders that they would face a heavy responsibility before God if they failed to act to control climate change. He said that while no one likes talking about enforceable international protocols like the Kyoto Protocol on climate change, there needs to be more concerted action if we are to prevent the collapse of the global economy which would cause pain, hardship and death for millions or even billions of people. To underscore his own commitment to reducing carbon emissions, the archbishop said that environmental auditors are looking at Anglican Church property along with his own house at Lambeth Palace in order to calculate the Anglican Church's carbon footprint.[10]

This is the kind of action all churches should be taking and the time for action is very short indeed. Scientists are adamant that unless carbon emissions are reduced by over 2.6% per annum during the next two decades, irreversible damage will be

10. Ruth Glendhill, 'Politicians will answer: Dr Williams said that global warming was a moral issue', *The Times*, March 29, 2006. www.timesonline.co.uk/politicians will answer/politics/29/03/ 2006.

done to the life-system of the planet. At the publication of a Report on climate change at the Royal Society on 30 January 2006, Rachel Warren of the Tyndall Centre for Climate Predictions and Research told the audience of scientists and policy-makers that governments have 20 years in which to act.[13]

13. Lewis Smith, '20 years to defuse climate disaster time bomb', *Irish Independent*, 31 January 2006, page 13.

# CHAPTER 1

# *The Atmosphere*

The atmosphere of planet earth is about 100 kilometres deep. The bulk of the gases which make up our atmosphere are found in the first five to ten kilometers. This very thin layer of gases sustains all life on earth. Energy from the sun, which is crucial for all life, reaches the earth through our atmosphere. If there was no atmosphere, life, as we know it, would not exist. The average temperature of the earth without its atmosphere would be around minus 18 degrees celsius. This would be too cold for life to thrive. It is because of the protective mantle of the atmosphere that the average global temperature of the earth is around plus 15 degrees celsius.[1]

The atmosphere also creates our climates, our clouds and our winds. The clouds produce rain which is a key element in our hydrological system, linking the atmosphere with the oceans. There are four distinct layers in the atmosphere. Starting at ground level, the troposphere extends 12 kilometres above the surface of the earth. It contains 80% of the gases in the atmosphere. The most important thing about this region of the atmosphere is its temperature gradient. This means that it is warmest at the bottom and cools by 6.5 degrees celsius at each kilometre above the ground. Above the troposphere we find the stratosphere. In contrast to the troposphere the stratosphere gets hotter as one moves up because it is rich in ozone which traps ultraviolet energy. The mesosphere lies 50 kilometres above the earth. The temperature here is minus 90 degrees celsius. It is the

---

1. In this section I repeat some of what I have already written in *Greening the Christian Millennium*, Dominican Publications, Dublin, 1999, pages 62-84.

coldest part of the atmosphere. Above the mesosphere lies the thermosphere which consists of a very thin layer of gas.[2]

Glacial periods, followed by shorter warm periods, have been a feature of world climate history for at least two million years – long before human activity could be blamed for bringing about climate change. During the last period of glaciation, which began about 120,000 years ago, much of Ireland was buried under one kilometre of ice. In some places the ice was so heavy that it pushed the earth's crust down into the mantle. Since the ice melted 12,000 years ago, the rebound of the earth's crust is still happening in some places.

Scientists point to three naturally occurring phenomena which account for these regularly recurring warming and cooling periods. The first phenomenon flows from the fact that the earth's orbit is more elliptical than circular. This means that, at certain times, the earth is closer or further away from the sun and this consequently impacts on the earth's climate. This means that the intensity of the sun's rays which reach the earth are markedly different throughout the year. Normally there is only a 6% difference in the sun's radiation if one compares the figures for January and July. When the orbit is fully elliptical the difference can range from 20% to 30% which is quite considerable. This phenomenon takes place about every 100,000 years.

The second phenomenon is related to the tilt in the earth's axis of rotation. This tilt is normally at 23.4 degrees but can vary from 21.8 to 24.4 degrees. This cycle determines where the sun's radiation falls and it takes 42,000 years to complete.

The third and final phenomenon is associated with a 'wobble' in the earth's rotational axis which occurs every 22,000 years. During this cycle the axis of the earth shifts from pointing to the polar star to pointing to a star called Vega. This affects the climatic intensity of the seasons, bringing mild summers and harsh, cold winters.

These three natural cycles are called the *Milankovitch* cycles

---

2. Tim Flannery, *The Weather Makers: The History and Future Impact of Climate Change*, Allen Lane (Penguin), London, 2005, page 20 -21.

after the Serbian scientist Milutin Milankovich who was the first
to use these naturally occurring phenomena to explain how ice
ages and warm inter-glacial periods come about naturally. His
theories were not well known because he wrote in Serbian. His
writings did not become available in English until the 1960s.

One of the most interesting aspects of the Milankovitch cycles
is that, even when they are synchronised, the annual amount of
solar radiation reaching the earth may be less than one tenth of
1% yet, it seems that such minute changes can stimulate the beginning of an ice age.[3] If we take these three processes working together, the earth's climate should at this point in time be moving
out of a warm inter-glacial period back into an ice age.

Sunspots can also affect localised climate changes. A lack of
sunspots is now thought to be responsible for the cold spell
which hit Europe during the late 17th and early 18th centuries
causing rivers like the Liffey and Thames to freeze regularly in
winter. This period is known as the Maunder minimum, after
the scientist who first drew attention to it.[4] Some scientists claim
that a cessation of sunspots activity could temporarily cause the
earth to cool. But they are quick to point out that it will only be a
respite from the ravages of man-made climate change.[5]

### Human Induced Climate Change

However, there is now a consensus among scientists, especially
those involved in the Intergovernmental Panel on Climate
Change (IPCC), that the current warming of the planet is due to
human activity. This is specifically attributed to the burning of
fossil fuels over the past two centuries since the beginning of the
industrial revolution. John Tyndall, a British physicist was the
first person to do any significant research in this area. In 1859 he
designed a machine called a spectrophotometer to study the
heat trapping properties of various gases. He discovered that

3. Tim Flannery, op. cit., pages 41-42.
4. Martin Rees, *Our Final Century; Will The Human Race Survive the
Twenty-First Century?* William Heinemann, London, 2003, page 106.
5. Stuart Clark, 'Saved by the SUN', *Newscientist*, 16 September 2006,
page 36.

oxygen and nitrogen, the gases which comprise most of the atmosphere, are transparent to both light and infra-red radiation. He also found that gases like carbon dioxide and methane, though found in much smaller quantities in the atmosphere, trap infrared heat. Tyndall realised that it was these gases that were responsible for determining the earth's climate. If these gases were not present, the average temperature of the planet would be around minus 18 degrees celsius. But because of the presence of the earth's protective mantle, which includes carbon dioxide, methane and other heat-absorbing gases, the average temperature of the earth is plus 15 degrees celsius which makes the earth very suitable for living organisms to thrive.

It took almost forty years for the Swedish chemist Svante Arrhenius to build on Tyndall's work. He asked whether the carbon dioxide which the industrial world was spewing into the atmosphere was adding to the carbon already there and what the consequence of this might be. In 1894, he set out to calculate what might happen to the earth's temperature if the level of carbon dioxide doubled. Living in a time before the advent of calculators or computers, he spent one year working on the calculations involved in the project. Finally, in December 1885, he produced a scientific paper for the Royal Swedish Academy of Sciences. His basic findings were that if the carbon levels in the atmosphere doubled the earth's climate would be affected and mean temperatures would rise gradually. He estimated that it would take 3,000 years of burning coal to double the concentration of carbon dioxide in the atmosphere.

During the following seven decades little work was done by scientists on whether human activity, especially burning fossil fuel, was changing the global climate. Some argued that the oceans would become a sink for any extra carbon in the atmosphere. Most scientists assumed that in recent earth history the proportion of gases in the atmosphere was more or less constant. However, great strides were made in forecasting weather, though usually in a fairly restricted area and forecasts were for shorter periods of time, no more than a day or so in advance.

Research on climate over the past 50 years has added significantly to our knowledge about climate change. Scientists have
better sources of data. This data originates from satellites, ice-
cores, seabed samples, weather records and dendrology, in addition to the data from the network of weather stations around
the world.

One important source of knowledge is gleaned from the ice
sheets which are found in both the Arctic and Antarctic regions.
Scientists can now take samples over one mile deep from ice-
sheets and discover all kinds of information about past climate
patterns. These ice cores can tell scientists the percentage of the
various gases in the atmosphere at any time during the past
400,000 years. This research has undermined one accepted tenet
of climatology which is that climate change happens very slowly.
One incidence of this is the rapid climate change which happened 12,000 years ago called Younger Dryas. This is associated
with the beautiful artic plant called Mountain Avens (*Dryas oc-
topetala*) which is found in the Burren region of Co Clare. The
earth, which had been warming for the previous few thousand
years, was snapped back into a very cold spell during the
Younger Dryas which lasted 1,200.[6]

Temperature data can be gleaned from the composition of
the ice sjeet and the ratio of gases to each other in the small air
bubbles that are found in the ice. Such data is pointing to the fact
that the earth is almost as warm now as at any time in the past
three and a half million years, a period known as the mid-
Pliocene warm period. The ice cores tell us that for the past
10,000 years, right up to the beginning of the industrial revolution 200 years ago, the average parts per million (ppm) of carbon
dioxide in the atmosphere was 280ppm. However, measurements taken at the Mauna Loa observatory in Hawaii in 1958 by
Dr Charles Keeling and his team found that there were 315ppm of
carbon dioxide in the atmosphere. In 2005, it was 378ppm and rising by 2ppm each year. It is estimated that there has been a 35%

6. Elizabeth Kolbert, 'The Climate of Man -1', *The New Yorker*, 25 April
2005, page 67.

increase in carbon dioxide since the beginning of the industrial revolution.[7] It is projected that by 2050 it will be over 500ppm.

Special Scientific Institutes such as The Goddard Institute for Space Studies (GISS) in New York are providing other tools which are deepening our understanding of how climate operates and what are the dynamics of climate change. GISS is an outpost for NASA and began as a planetary research station. Today one of its main functions is to provide information about climate. The 150 scientists at GISS work on different aspects of climate forecasting. They study the oceans, global vegetation, the atmosphere, the movement of clouds and rainfall patterns. The results of these studies are expressed as mathematical formulae which can be fed into a supercomputer. Their recent climate change model, based on the results of their research, is called Model E. It has 125,000 lines of a computer programme. This is just one of the computer climate models in operation today. There are 15 other computer models in various parts of the world, like the Postdam Institute Impact Research in Germany. Institutes like these provide much of the data for UN's Intergovernmental Panel on Climate Change (IPCC).[8]

In order to test the accuracy of these models in predicting the future of climate, the researchers run them backwards to see if the findings match the actual weather patterns of the past, which are determined from other sources such as written documentation, dendrology, ice cores etc. The climate model at GISS factored in data from the volcanic eruption at Mount Pinatubo on the island of Luzon in the Philippines in 1991, which injected over 20 million tons of gas into the atmosphere. This condensed into tiny sulfate droplets which reflected sunlight back into space. Model E's calculations about the impact of this event on the global climate came within 900th of a degree of accuracy.[9] This is very accurate indeed.

---

7. Robin Mckie, 'Condemned to death by degrees if we fail to act', *The Observer*, 26 June 2005, A1.
8. Elizabeth Kolbert, 'The Climate of Man – 2', *The New Yorker*, 2 May 2005, page 67.
9. Ibid 68.

Recent research on Arctic seabed samples indicate that 55 million years ago the climate was much warmer and had a year round average temperature of 74 degrees celsius. Scientists claim, from their analysis of the seabed samples, that until now the scientific community has underestimated the potential of heat-trapping gases to warm the Arctic. By examining the seabed samples the scientists can now understand the various cycles of heating and cooling that have occurred over the last 45 million years. This study would seem to support the theory that the cold and hot periods in climate history are as a result of greenhouse gases primarily.[10]

What has brought about the recent changes in the percentage of the various gases in the atmosphere? During the past two centuries and a half, humans have begun to utilise fossil fuel in a more extensive way. Initially coal was used to power the beginnings of the industrial revolution in England, Continental Europe and latterly the United States. After the discovery of oil in the 1880s, oil gradually replaced coal, primarily because it is more versatile. It was also the preferred fuel for powering the internal combustion engine in cars, trucks, trains, airplanes and ships. Natural gas, most of which is methane, is now used widely in industry and for domestic use. It will probably be the most important fuel in the early part of the 21st century.

As the 20th century progressed, particularly after World War II, human beings began to use more and more hydrocarbons as they bought cars and used fossil fuel to generate electricity. In fact there was a sixteen-fold increase in the burning of fossil fuel in the 20th century.[11] As more and more fossil fuel was burned the change in the percentage of gases in the atmosphere became more pronounced and the atmosphere began to heat up.

A study carried out by scientists from the University of East Anglia in Britain found that the late 20th century was the hottest

10. Andrew C. Rivkin, 'Studies Portray Tropical Arctic in Distant Past', *The New York Times*, 1 June 2006, www.nytimes.com/2006/06/01/science/earth01climate.html page 1-3.
11. Tim Flannery, *The Weather Makers*, op cit, page 77.

period in the northern hemisphere since the year 800 AD. The scientists used data from a variety of sources including tree ring-data, ice cores, the chemical composition of sea shells, and historical documents in this study. Dr Timothy Osborn, co-author of the study, wrote 'the 20th century stands out as having unusually widespread warmth, compared to all the natural warming and cooling episodes during the past 12,000 years'.[12]

The reason why global warming is called the 'greenhouse effect' is simple. Most of the solar radiation is absorbed by the earth's surface. Some is reflected back and is dissipated into space. However, some long-wave radiation is captured by greenhouse gases like carbon dioxide, methane and others. These gases act like the glass in a greenhouse and retain the heat. All of the above are part of the normal global processes, which regulate climate conditions and maintain the warmth and moisture that are essential for life. As long as the percentages of the various gases in the atmosphere remain more or less constant, an equilibrium is established which ensures the continuity of the present living world.

There are a number of other gases responsible for climate change besides carbon dioxide ($CO_2$). These include methane ($CH_4$), nitrous oxide ($N_2O$), hydrofluorocarbons (HFCs), perfluorocarbons (PFCs) and sulphur hexofluoride. Methane is produced by fossil fuel extraction, cattle farming, rice growing, landfills and more recently by melting permafrost. The average life time of methane in the atmosphere is about 12 years. This means it has a much shorter life time than carbon dioxide.

Nitrous oxide is a minor greenhouse gas. Its concentration in the atmosphere is 0.3ppm and, its present level is about 16% greater than in pre-industrial times. However it has a long atmospheric lifespan of around 115 years.[13] Its main sources are from agriculture, the chemical industry and the burning of fossil fuels.

---

12. Steve Connor, 'World is at its warmest for a millennium', *The Independent*, February 10, 2006. www.news.independent.co.uk/environment/article344513 11/02/2006
13. John Haughton, 2004, *Global Warming*, CUP, page 44.

Chlorofluorocarbons or CFCs are synthetically created chemicals which were widely used in refrigeration because of their safety and versatility until it was discovered in the 1970s that they were destroying the ozone layer of the atmosphere. Once released into the atmosphere the chlorine can take 5 years to reach the ozone layer. Once there it attacks and destroys the ozone. In 1985, the British Antarctic team lead by Joe Farman discovered that ozone had been stripped from huge areas of the atmosphere over Antarctica. Since ozone absorbs harmful ultraviolet radiation from the sun, ozone depletion would have enormous consequence for human welfare and the natural world. The serious nature of ozone depletion was recognised by many governments in the early 1980s and it led to the signing of the Montreal Protocol in 1987. CFCs are also greenhouse gases. Even though they have a miniscule presence in the atmosphere a single CFC molecule has 5,000 to 10,000 times more global warming effect than a carbon dioxide molecule.

Since the Montreal Protocol, CFCs have been replaced by other halocarbons, and hydroflurocarbons. Neither of these chemicals contain chlorine or bromine and therefore do not destroy the ozone layer. Their global warming effect is also much less than CFCs but if they continue to be manufactured in increasing bulk their impact as global warming gases will increase.

Under every current scenario put forward by the Intergovernmental Panel on Climate Change (IPCC) the average global temperature is expected to continue to rise. They estimate that the increase in surface temperatures will range between 1.4 and 5.8 degrees celsius over the 21st century. In May 2006, researchers at the Centre for Ecology and Hydrology in Britain, claimed that these figures are conservative estimates by at least 2 degrees celsius. According to Peter Cox, the director of the Centre, the initial calculations were made on the basis of the well-known fact that carbon dioxide warms the planet by insulating it like a blanket. What is less well known is that as the earth warms more carbon dioxide is released from both soil and oceans, thus increasing further the amount of carbon dioxide in the atmosphere. The knock-on effect of this is a further warming of the earth.[14]

Even if the changes in temperature are to be kept at the lower level of the scale, we still need to understand the dynamics of climate change, its potential consequence, and what we can do to mitigate its worst effects.

Some of these changes could mean that some places might actually become colder than they are at present. If, for example, the Gulf Stream is interfered with as a result of global warming, then Ireland, Britain and Northern Europe could be plunged into a mini-ice age. The Gulf Stream is responsible for bringing about one third of the heat of the sun to Western Europe. There are records that the Gulf Stream slowed down and stopped in the past and the processes which caused this are now better understood. As the warmer water from the Gulf Stream moves north into the colder regions of the Atlantic, it sinks because it is saltier and therefore heavier than the surrounding water. This in turn draws more warm salty water northwards. If fresh water from melting glaciers dilutes the saltiness of the Gulf Stream, its warming impact on Western Europe could be terminated or diminished.[15]

At present global warming in the Arctic is accelerating through a phenomenon known the *Albedo* effect. *Albedo* comes from the Latin word for whiteness. During the Arctic winter the area of sea ice expands and the increased white surface reflects the sun's light back into space. The *Albedo* effect is measured around 0.8 or 0.9. When the ice melts the water absorbs the sun's energy and the *albedo* drops down to less than 0.1 to 0.07. Commenting on this change, Elizabeth Kolbert of *The New Yorker* put it succinctly when she wrote that it is like 'replacing the best reflector with the worst reflector'.[16] Here we encounter the notion of feedback loops. As more sea ice is lost to oceans,

14. Ian Sample, 'Global warming predictions are underestimated say scientists', *The Guardian*, 23 May 2006, page 3.
15. Tim Flannery, op. cit, page 60.
16. Elizabeth Kolbert, *The New Yorker*, 25 April 2005, page 64.

more energy is absorbed by them which, in turn, heats up the planet. According to Elizabeth Kolbert the *albedo* factor is the main reason why the Arctic ocean is heating up so rapidly.[17]

Despite a few remaining skeptics and the usual vested interest groups, especially those who have invested heavily in the fossil fuel industry, there is now a broad consensus among scientists that climate change is happening. We therefore need to understand what the consequences will be for humans, other species and the planet. Finally, we need to know what we can do to prevent the worst case scenarios from taking shape.

## Time Scales Involved in Climate Change

As I wrote on page 16, until very recently it was assumed that the climate would not change abruptly; that it would take decades or even centuries for a major climate change to happen. This assumption has been challenged in recent times. Scientists from Trinity College, Dublin found that there was a profound change in the local climate in Glendalough, Co Wicklow about 11,500 years ago. Using pollen grains extracted from the sediment in the lakes, the scientists found that the climate changed from a tundra-like condition to a mild climate in a period of 7 years. Initially, there were no trees, merely grasses, heathers and some juniper bushes. Within a decade, trees – birch, oak, elm and pine – were established in the area. John Haslett is the statistician for the project. He is quoted as saying, 'the speed at which this happened (climate change) is gobsmacking. It may not have happened in 24 hours, like in (the film) *The Day After Tomorrow* but the science in the film is correct. (A major climate change) had to do with the Gulf Stream switching on and off.'[18]

In Chapter two we will see that the current situation in Greenland is very similar to what it was in Wicklow, 11,500 years ago. Could we be witnessing abrupt climate change happening at this point in history?

---

17. Ibid.
18. Jan Battles, 'How Wicklow went from artic to mild in seven years', *The Sunday Times*, 25 June 2006, page 6.

# CHAPTER 2

# Climate Change and Extreme Weather

*More frequent and violent storms*

Hurricanes of great ferocity, such as Gilbert which caused major devastation in Jamaica and along the coast of Mexico in 1988, may not be caused by global warming but they are exacerbated by it. The same is true of hurricane Andrew, which tore through the State of Florida in 1992. Hurricane Mitch slammed into Central America in October 1999, causing devastating floods and triggering mudslides which caused the deaths of over 10,000 on the Caribbean coast of Venezuela.[1] The year 2004 produced four major hurricanes in the Caribbean and the Southern United States causing numerous deaths and massive damage to property. It is estimated that the cost of the damage done by these storms was in excess of $45 billion.

In 2004, Pacific nations like Japan, Taiwan, Korea and the Philippines experienced unusually severe typhoons. For the first time in recent history a hurricane developed in the Southern Atlantic. The 90 miles per hour winds of hurricane Catarina left a trail of destruction in Brazil causing approximately twelve deaths. As global warming increases, scientists are predicting that tropical storms will increase both in power and in number.[2]

In 2005, the greatest number of hurricanes appeared in the Atlantic-Caribbean area since records began, beating the previous record which was set in 1969. Hurricane Katrina was one that will be remembered for decades as it destroyed the city of New Orleans and much of the Gulf Coast of Mississippi and Alabama. Almost one and a half million people were displaced

---

1. Sir David King, 'Clean air act', *The Guardian Supplement*, 24 November 2004, page 15.
2. 'G 8 Summit', *The Independent*, 5 July 2005, page 7.

and 1,800 lost their lives. The storm breached the levees on the Mississippi river and because New Orleans is situated 6 feet below sea level, water from the river poured into the city. The projected cost of the clean-up and rehabilitation of its citizens is estimated at $100 billion. This does not include the human misery which resulted from the storm.

Within one month, another powerful hurricane called Rita lashed into the coast of Louisiana and Texas. At one point this was a category 5 hurricane and many feared that it would hit the oil ports of Galveston and Port Arthur and disrupt the oil business there. Once again, more than one million people were forced to leave their homes in Galveston and Houston. The state and federal authorities were better prepared for hurricane Rita, yet it still caused massive damage, shattering windows and bringing down power cables. The logistics involved in the evacuation of people were extremely difficult. Many people were stranded for hours on the highways. Thousands of motorists ran out of fuel as did numerous service stations. A bus carrying 38 nursing home residents from Houston caught fire and exploded just south of Dallas. At least 24 people died in the accident. Once again, rain and the storm surge from hurricane Rita breached the levees in New Orleans, setting back the rebuilding programme by four weeks.

On 19 October 2005, another major hurricane called Wilma formed in the Atlantic and headed for Mexico and Florida. At an early stage, Wilma turned into an extremely dangerous category 5 hurricane. Wilma was the 21st major storm of the 2005 season. On 23 October 2005, having done huge damage on the Yucatan coast of Mexico, Wilma crashed into Florida killing at least six people and leaving three million homes without power. Insurers estimated that the total bill for cleaning up and rebuilding Florida would be in the region of $9 billion. Wilma was the eighth hurricane to hit Florida in 15 months. Hurricane Wilma struck Cuba in October 2005 leading to the evacuation of 640,000 people. In Cuba, rescuers used scuba gear, inflatable rafts and amphibious vehicles to pull nearly 250 people from their flooded homes in Havana.

Tropical storms also take place in the Pacific Ocean. In 1970, one of the worst storms of the 20th century caused the death of 250,000 people in low lying areas of Bangladesh. Another major typhoon hit Bangladesh in 1999 causing serious damage and loss of life. In 1993, thousands of people were killed by mudslides which followed a typhoon that hit the east coast of southern Luzon in the Philippines.

While one cannot say for certain that a particular storm is a direct result of global warming, it is clear that warmer temperatures and raised ocean levels will cause huge damage to coastal areas in the future. The available scientific evidence indicates that it is likely that global warming will make – and possibly already is making – those hurricanes that do form more destructive than otherwise they would have been.

There is also empirical evidence to show that hurricanes are becoming more intense. The magazine *Nature* published a study by Kerry Emanuel, a hurricane scientist at Massachusetts Institute of Technology (MIT), which concluded that hurricanes have doubled in intensity over the past 30 years.[3] Naomi Oreskes of the University of California, San Diego, wrote an essay for *Nature* in which she analysed 928 articles published in other scientific journals between 1993 and 2003. She discovered that none of the articles disagreed with the present consensus position which argues that human activity is causing a rise in global temperatures.[4]

The insurance companies are also aware that climate change is happening. In 2000, one of the largest insurance companies in the world – Munich-Re – published a report claiming that 'climate change could trigger worldwide losses totaling many hundreds of billions of US dollars per year. Most countries can expect their losses to range from a few tenths of a percent of the

3. *New York Times*, 11 September 2005. www.nytimes.com/2005/09/11opinion
4. Robin Meckie, 'Condemned to death by degrees if we fail to act', *The Observer*, 7 July 2005, A2.

GNP per year; and certain countries, especially Small Island States could face losses extending to 10%.'[5]

*Extreme Weather in Britain and Ireland*
Extreme weather will also affect Ireland and Britain if global warming continues as predicted. A report sponsored by the British government and climate change scientists was released at the end of April 2002. It stated that the world temperature was warmer in the first three months of the year than at any time in the past one thousand years. This report predicts that the weather in Britain and Ireland will become warmer and more unstable. In November 2002 there was widespread flooding in Dublin, Cork, and Co Meath. These once-in-30-year floods now come much more often.

Areas that expected to be flooded every 50 years can now expect that they will be flooded for 9 years out of 10 by 2080. Storms and heavy seas will batter coastal areas during winter much more than previously. Many predict that the summers in Ireland and Britain will be longer and drier. There will be an average increase in temperature of more than 0.25 celsius each decade. The top temperatures in the south of England could reach 40 degrees celsius. Such a major climate change will have a huge impact on Irish agriculture and on the Irish landscape.[6]

Other analysts believe that the future in Ireland may not be so rosy.[7] They base their predictions on the fact that the melting of the Arctic ice cap may interfere with or suspend the Gulf Stream which is responsible for Northern Europe's temperate climate. As I mentioned before, the warm salt water flowing north in the Gulf Stream could be diluted with run-offs of fresh water from the Greenland ice fields and thus the salt water would not sink towards the bottom. This would result in slow-

5. *Solidarity with the Victims of Climate Change*, January 2002, World Council of Churches, page 9.
6. Ann Cahill, 'Days of drought and deluge loom', *The Irish Examiner*, 1 May 2002, page 5.
7. William Calvin, *A Brain for All Seasons, Evolution and Abrupt Climate Change*, University of Chicago Press, 2002.

ing down or stopping the 'converyer belt' altogether, which would have a major adverse impact on global climates This would leave Ireland, and much of Northern Europe, much colder than it is now. Not a welcome scenario! The complete shut down of the thermohaline circulation of the Gulf Stream in this century is very unlikely but a slowing down is certainly on the cards.

## Melting of Glaciers

There are about 160,000 glaciers on earth. Only about 40 have been monitored closely during the past 30 years. Many of these have been melting at a greater rate during the past 20 years due to global warming. There is every reason to fear that as warming continues the glaciers will begin to move and disintegrate at an increasing level. The reason for this acceleration is that melt-water from the glacier's surface seeps down through cracks on to the bedrock and this water begins to act as a lubricant, thus speeding up the movement of the glacier.

Adrian Luckman of the University of Wales, Swansea, and a team of scientists, have been studying two of the largest glaciers in Greenland, Kangerdlugssuaq and Helhelm. These are about 300 kilometres apart and drain one tenth of the surface of Greenland. They discovered that during 2004 and 2005 these glaciers have doubled their speed to about 14 kilometres annually. In 1998, scientists noticed a similar increase in speed in the Jakobshavn glacier in Greenland, which is the fastest-moving glacier in the world. Using satellite images the scientists calculated that the two glaciers, Kangerdlugssuaq and Helhelm, are now depositing 100 cubic kilometers of ice into the ocean each year. Writing in the journal *Geophysical Research Letters*, Luckman stated that 'these glaciers, behaving in a similar way within a few years of each other after a long period of stability, implies both a common cause – climate change – and a high probability that other Greenland glaciers will respond likewise'.[8]

Snow and ice on the eastern Himalayas has decreased by

---

8. 'Glacier Slip-Sliding Away', *Newscientist*, 11 February 2006, page 7.

30% since the 1970s.[9] Within the next five years as many as forty lakes will have been formed by melting ice high up in the Himalayas, especially in Nepal and Bhutan. These lakes could burst their banks and cause devastation in the lowland valleys. According to Paul Brown of *The Guardian*, 'there are thought to be hundreds more such liquid time bombs in India, Pakistan Afghanistan, Tibet and China'.[10] The situation is rendered more dangerous by the fact that many of these lakes are in geologically unstable areas. A sizeable earthquake could trigger a disaster.

The impact of melting glaciers on agriculture could also be catastrophic. If the glaciers melt on the Himalayas this will affect the melt waters of The Ganges, Bramaputra, Mekong and Yangtse rivers. Over one quarter of humanity depend on these rivers for their food production.[11]

In South America, Peru has lost about one third of its glaciers in the past thirty years. The consequences of this could be catastrophic for Peruvians, as most of the population live in the large cities like Lima. Lima's water supply comes from glacier-fed rivers. If, in two decades, the glaciers on the Peruvian side of the Andes have melted, the 7 million inhabitants of Lima will be starved for water.[12]

Iceland is one country where glaciers are systematically studied and the condition of glaciers is a topic of general conversation. In the autumn, at the end of the summer-melt season, volunteers working with the Icelandic Glaciological Society survey the 300 plus glaciers and file reports on their condition. The growth in Iceland's glaciers in the 1970s and 1980s was often quoted by those dismissing global warming. However, in the mid 1990s the glaciers began to decline. The decline was slow at first but then it gathered pace. For example, a glacier called

---

9. David Adam, 'UN urged to save glaciers and reefs', *The Guardian*, 16 March 2006, page 9.
10. Paul Brown, 'Global warming melts glaciers and produces many unstable lakes', *The Guardian*, 17 April 2002
11. Elizabeth Kolbert, 'The Climate of Man', op. cit., page 71.
12. Michael McCarthy, 'Waiting in the wings: the other leaders who must take a giant leap for the planet', *The Independent*, 5 July 2005, page 5.

Solheimajokull began to recede slowly in 1996 and the loss for that year was 10 feet. In 1997, it increased to 33 feet and by 1998 it had reached 98 feet. In 2003, it shrank by 302 feet and by 2004 it was a further 285 feet back. In total this glacier was 11,000 feet shorter in 2004 than in 1994. The situation at present is so desperate that some climate models predict that Iceland will be glacier free within 150 years.[13]

On a global level glaciers are in retreat because of global warming. However, in some situations, particularly the maritime glaciers in Scandinavia, they were maintaining equilibrium or even expanding slightly during the last decades of the 20th century. Writing in the *International Journal of Climatology*, Rowan Fealy and John Sweeney attribute this change to atmospheric variability in the North Atlantic, due to an increase in the intensities of winds coming off the sea. This in turn prevents the warm air from the south from entering into the area. Change in winter rainfall patterns also added to the maritime glaciers. However, since the 1980s the Scandinavian maritime glaciers have been shrinking and this is expected to increase as global warming heats up the planet.[14] Global warming is causing the same phenomenon in Greenland. While glaciers are melting at an astonishing rate at the edge of the ice cap, the ice cap itself is thickening in some areas due to increased snow falls during the winter months. The Norwegian scientist, Ola Johannessen, whose team won the European Commission's Descartes prize in 2005, is appalled when 'right-wing think-tanks' in the US use their data to counter the global warming claims. In May 2005, the Competitive Enterprise Institute, which is funded by Exxon Mobile to the tune of $2 million, ran a series of TV advertisements portraying the notion of glaciers shrinking as a myth. The

13. Elizabeth Kolbert 'The Climate of Man', *The New Yorker*, 25 April 2006, page 70.
14. Rowan Fealy and John Sweeney, 'Detection of a possible change point in atmospheric variability in the north Atlantic and its effects on Scandinavian Glacier mass Balance', *International Journal of Climatology*, 2005.

commercial ended with the slogan 'Carbon dioxide – they call it pollution – we call it life.'[15]

*Damaging Winter Tourist Industry*
Melting glaciers will also have a damaging impact on tourism in ski resorts. In Switzerland alone, up to half the ski resorts will be affected. The situation in Germany, Italy and Austria will be even worse. These countries do not expect to have any snow within 10 years. Because the lower reaches of the mountains now lack snow in the resorts, the industry is using artificial snow. This contains fungicides, salts and millions of cubic metres of water and thus is having a negative impact on soils and plants.

According to Sonja Wipf, a scientist based at the Swiss Federal Institute for Snow and Avalanche Research at Davos, 'global warming is affecting the whole ecology in the area'. The blue berry crop in both the Davos and Klosters area was wiped out in 2005 because, 'spring frosts are arriving later and later and this causes serious damage to many plants at crucial stages in their development'.[16] The melting of the Alpine glaciers will increase the stress on many Alpine plant species to the point that many will become extinct. Climate change could send European tourists flocking to the UK and Ireland to escape unbearably hot continental summers, according to David Viner, a researcher at the University of East Anglia's Climate Research Unit in Norwich.[17]

*Permafrost*
When soil or rock remains below 32 degrees Fahrenheit, in other words in a frozen state, for two or more years it is called permafrost. It contrasts with soils which freeze during the cold winter but thaw out in the late spring or early summer. There is now

15. Frank McDonald, 'Global Warming: the front line', *The Irish Times*, *Weekend Review*, 24 June 2006, page 3.
16. Jennifer Forsyth and Nelson Graves, 'Steep Decline', *The Guardian*, Society/Guardian/Environment, 15 2006, page 8.
17. www.travel.guardian.co.uk/print/0,,329540820-104894,html

evidence that the permafrost which has gripped hundreds of millions of acres in the Arctic region for over one hundred thousand years, is beginning to melt. As the permafrost melts huge fissures open up in the ground. These are called thermokarsts. These thermokarsts are appearing regularly in places like Fairbanks in Alaska. The knock-on effect of this thawing has been that many houses are no longer habitable and roads have been destroyed.

Unfortunately, melting permafrost holds more bad news. Until very recently the temperature was so cold that when trees or other organic matter died it did not fully decompose. New plants grew out of partially decomposed matter. Over time this layer of partly decomposed organic matter was pushed down into the permafrost layer where it remained for millennia in a frozen state. This process is called 'cryoturbation'. Now with the melting of the permafrost this organic matter is beginning to rot and, in the process, release both carbon dioxide and methane into the atmosphere. It is not known how much organic matter is stored in this way across the arctic region. Some estimates put the figure as high as 400 billion metric tonnes.[18]

18. Elizabeth Kolbert, ' The Climate of Man 1', *The New Yorker*, April 25, 2005, page 61.

CHAPTER 3

# Climate Change, the Oceans
# and the Living World

*Rising Sea Levels*

During most of the last ice age, which began 120,000 ago and began to warm up about 15,000 years ago, the oceans were at least 100 metres lower than they are today. As the climate warmed the ice-caps in Europe and North America melted, raising the level of the oceans. About 8,000 years ago, the level stabilised to much the same level as it was 50 years ago. Now things are changing again: at the moment it is estimated that sea levels are rising at 3mm per year.[1] The 2001 Report from the UN's Intergovernmental Panel on Climate Change predicted that the rise in sea-level could be between four inches and three feet by the year 2100.[2] This figure does not include any contribution from either the Greenland or Antarctic ice-sheets and so is a conservative estimate.

Projected temperatures in Greenland and in Antarctic are already above the global average by one to three degrees celsius. If we continue to use fossil fuels in the way we have in recent decades, and if the Greenland ice cap melted, this would lead to a rise in sea levels of at least six metres. Previously it was though that this might take 1,000 years but recent research has changed these calculations considerably. In 2002, for example, it was discovered that the Greenland and the Arctic ice-cap contracted by a record 1 million kilometers which was the largest contraction to date. However, two years later in 2004, scientists discovered

---

1. John von Radowitz, 'Glacier melt rate has doubled in five years', *Irish Examiner*, February 17, 2006, page 9.
2. Elizabeth Kolbert, 'The Climate of Man –', *The New Yorker*, April 25, 2005, page 68.

that Greenland glaciers were melting at 10 times the rate that was previous projected.[3]

In the past 40 years, the Antarctic and Artic have warmed faster than anywhere else in the world, according to Alan Thrope, the chief executive of Britain's Natural Environment Research Council. In March 2002, scientists in the Antarctica revealed that the Larsen B ice shelf had disappeared from the map releasing 500 million, billion tonnes of fresh water into the sea. Glaciologists were taken aback by the speed with which the area disintegrated. It took only thirty-one days. In 2005, the head of the British Antarctic Survey, Professor Chris Rapley announced that the huge West Antarctic ice sheet may be beginning to disintegrate. If this happened it would mean that sea levels would rise by 16 feet from this event alone.[4]

In March 2006, a research team from the University of Colorado, using satellite data, estimated that the ice sheet in the Antarctic was losing up to 36 cubic miles of ice every year. This is an extremely significant finding. For example, a city like Los Angeles only uses one cubic mile of water each year. The bulk of this loss, close to 35 cubic miles, is happening on the West Antarctic ice sheet. Studies done by the International Panel on Climate Change (IPCC) in 2001 predicted that the Antarctic ice sheet would gain mass in the 21st century. Their reason was that snow levels would increase as the area heated up. But this may not be correct as it overlooks the dynamic between the changes in the interior region of the continent and the coastal areas.[5]

The reasons why the ice-fields in the Antarctic are breaking up so rapidly is that the temperature in the area has increased by 2.5 degrees celsius in the past fifty years. Temperatures are rising more quickly in the Arctic and Antarctic because the *albedo* effect is reduced when ice flows and snow melt are replaced by ocean water. As we have seen in chapter one, the *albedo* is at its

---

3. Tim Flannery, op. cit., page 144.
4. Michael McCarthy, 'Climate poses increased threat, admits Blair', *The Independent*, 30 January 2006. www.news.independent.co.uk/environment/article341944 30/01/2006 page 1 of 2
5 ibid.

highest when ice is covered with snow and at its lowest when
the ice melts leaving only sea water.[6] The decline in the ice sheet
has had a detrimental effect on wild life, especially on polar
bears. They find it much more difficult to hunt seals, because the
ice cracks beneath their feet. Since they are no longer able to catch
seals, they face an uncertain future and possibly extinction.

Scientists at the US National Snow and Ocean Data Centre in
Colorado fear that the Arctic region is locked into a destructive
cycle with warmer air melting more ice which in turn further
warms the air. 2006 was the fourth year in a row in which the
melting ice was greater than average. It increased the overall decline in sea ice by 8%, up from 6.4% in 2002.[7] Walt Meier, a researcher at the US National Snow and Ice Data Center in
Colorado, reported that their research showed that as of March
2006 the area covered by sea ice in the Arctic area was down
300,000 square kilometers on the previous year. At that rate of
melting experts predict that the Arctic might be ice-free by 2030.[8]

The Greenland ice field is 3 kilometres thick and covers 1.7
million square kilometres. Research published early in 2006
showed that there was a dramatic rise in the ice being lost from
the field. In 1996, it was 90 cubic kilometres. This jumped to 224
cubic kilometres by 2005.[9] If the Greenland ice sheet melted
completely it would raise global sea levels by 23 feet or 7 metres.[10]

In 2005, scientists warned that global warming in the Arctic
might be accelerating out of control as new data revealed that
the floating cap of sea ice had shrunk to probably its smallest in
at least a century and probably much longer. Satellite images in
March 2006 revealed that Arctic winter sea ice was down
300,000 square kilometers on the previous year. When a variety

6. Elizabeth Kolbert, 'The Climate of Man', The New Yorker, April 25,
2005, page 64.
7. David Adam, 'Artic meltdown just decades away, scientists warn',
Sydney Morning Herald, www.smh.com.au/news/world/arctic-melt-
down../30/09/2005
8. David Adam, 'Meltdown fear as Arctic ice cover falls to record winter
low', The Guardian, May 15, 2006, page 12.
9. John von Radowitz, op.cit.,page 9.
10. ibid

of data is fed into the most sophisticated climate models some scientists are finding that there will not be perennial sea-ice in the Arctic by 2080. The seasonal sea-ice that forms in the winter will still be found. The summers, however, will be ice free.[11]

*Thermal Expansion of Water*

The main reason for the rise in sea levels is the thermal expansion of the ocean water. As the atmosphere warms up over decades and even centuries, there is a gradual transfer of thermal energy from the atmosphere to the oceans. As water heats up its volume expands. The contribution of thermal expansion will differ from place to place. Thermal expansion will be much more significant at the tropics than in the temperate zone. A typical rule of thumb has been set out by Professor John Houghton. He writes: 'At 5 degrees celsius (a typical temperature at high latitudes), a rise of 1 degree celsius causes an increase of water volume of about 1 part in 10,000 and at 25 degrees celsius (typical of tropical latitudes), the same temperature rise of 1 degree celsius increases the volume by about 3 parts in 10,000.[12] The rate of expansion will not be uniform. The top layer of the ocean will heat up first. Researchers at the World Data Center For Oceanography have compiled data records spanning 50 years on the warming of the oceans. The data has come from research institutes, naval vessels, submarines, merchant ships and satellites. They factored into a climate model 7 million observations and deduced that the top 10,000 feet of the world's oceans have been warming by an average of .037 degrees celsius since 1955. It may take a much longer period for the warmer water to work its way right through the vast body of the oceans. Still this finding is alarming because of the damage it will do to life in the oceans.[13] Furthermore, once the process begins it is more or less irreversible. It may take a few hundred years for it to be concluded but the actions we are taking today will set in train a

11. Elizabeth Kolbert, 'The Climate of Man – 1', *The New Yorker*, 25 April 2005, page 65.
12. John Haughton, *Global Warming*, op.cit. page 46.
13. Colin Woodard, 'Warming up the Seas', *E The Environmental Magazine*, July / August 2005, page 38.

process that will continue into the future and affect multiple generations.

## Consequence of ocean rise

Even if we move back from that figure to a mere rise of 10cm in oceans levels by 2030, it will have a negative impact on the lives of tens of millions of people. Firstly, more than half the population of the world lives in coastal areas which are often heavily populated and have some of the richest agricultural lands. In Bangladesh, a country with a population of 144,319,628, about one half of its agricultural land would be lost if the sea levels rose by a half a metre. Bangladeshis would be forced to migrate from the affected areas in their tens of millions.

In 1970 in Bangladesh about one quarter of a million people lost their lives in rains and sea surges caused by a typhoon. 100,000 were lost in a similar storm in 1991. Protecting the coast from sea surge is simple not an option. Secondly, and equally important is the fact that most of the productive farm land is found in the delta. This farm land would be lost by erosion and the intrusion of salt water into the fresh water aquifers, making parts of the coastline uninhabitable. So where will the millions of ecological refugees from Bangladesh go?

Bangladesh will not be the only country affected. Similar dynamics will operate on the Nile delta. Around twenty per cent of Egypt's arable land and more than 7 million of the population live in the delta. Low lying islands in the Indian Ocean like the Maldives and the Marshall Islands as well as Tuvalu, Kiribati, Palau, Gonga, Mauru and Cook Islands in the Pacific, many of which are less than three metres above sea level, will be adversely affected. Even a small rise in sea levels will adversely affect their fresh water supplies which are like a thin lens and therefore are very vulnerable to sea water intrusion into their fresh water reserves. For this reason, these island communities will run out of clean fresh water and thus become uninhabitable long before they are flooded. The Philippines, Indonesia, Thailand, Egypt and China would also be affected, creating tens of millions of environmental refugees.

The last time the earth was 5 degrees fahrenheit warmer was 3 million years ago. The oceans were 80 feet higher. If this were to happen in the next 200 to 300 years many cities on the east coast of the US, including New York, Philadelphia, Washington and Miami would be flooded. Most of the state of Florida would be lost to the seas.[14]

A rise in sea levels could be very costly for Ireland since many of our major cities are situated along the sea coast. These include Dublin, Cork, Waterford, Limerick, Galway, Sligo and Derry. Even a raise of 0.5 of a metre will take a toll on infrastructure in many of these cities. Railway lines that run along the sea shore will have to be relocated. Key areas of infrastructure will have to be protected. But building defences against the sea is costly and also hazardous, as was evident during the flooding of New Orleans in 2005.

During the ice age there was an ice cap of more than 1 kilometre over much of the northern part of Ireland which depressed the crust of the earth. As the earth in that area is still rebounding, rises in the level of the oceans have only kept pace with this phenomenon. In the southern part of Ireland it is different because they were not so comprehensively affected by the last ice age. This means that this area will be more susceptible to coastal erosion and floods from rises in the level of the seas. According to Dr Kieran R. Hickey the current level of coastal erosion is between 1 and 2 metres. Securing our coasts against global warming will cost a lot of money. Dr Hickey is critical of the government for shelving the extensive report on coastal zone management strategy designed by the consultants Brady, Shipman and Martin.[15]

This impact of climate change on the crust of the earth has been researched in recent years. One prominent scientist, Bill McGuire, is professor of geological hazards at University College

---

14. Jim Hansen, 'The Threat to the Planet', *New York Review*, 13 July 2006, page 13.
15. Dr Kieran R. Hickey, 'Sea-Level Rise Will Cost Ireland Billions', *The Local Planet*, November 2005-February 2006. page 38.

London. He believes that climate change and the subsequent melting of glaciers and rise in sea levels has historically led to changes in the crust of the earth and triggered either volcanic explosions or earthquakes. He makes the point that as ice-sheets, that have pinned down volcanoes and active faults melted the earth's crust bounced back and gave rise to increased seismic and volcanic activity. He points to the increase in volcanic activity in Iceland at the beginning of the present inter-glacial period 10,000 years ago. He believes that the same process may be happening now with the melting of glaciers and the rise in sea-levels.[16]

## Global Warming and Marine Life

Warmer seas have an impact on the marine life. In Alaska's Bering Sea, capelin, herring and other coldwater fish are becoming much scarcer. With warming water fish like albacore are beginning to appear further north.

Global Warming is also causing massive changes on coral reefs. After rainforests, these are some of the most biologically rich life-systems on the planet. They are home to over 9 million kinds of plants and animals, including possibly a quarter of the world's fish. As global warming increases and warms up the surface of the ocean, the coral polyps that form the reefs begin to die back leaving only the white corals. This is called coral bleaching. In 1998, when temperatures reached a record high, especially in Asia, 90% of the coral reefs were affected by bleaching. If disasters like 1998 were to happen each year because of global warming, the survival of coral reefs globally would be at risk.[17] Dr Tim Flannery, the director of the South Australian Museum, states in his book, *The Weather Makers*, that Australia's great coral reef is particularly at risk. 'Visitors travelling to Queensland by 2050 may see the Great Stumpy Reef.'[18] The

16. Bill McCuire, 'Earth, Fire and Fury', *NewScientist*, 27 May 2006, pages 32-36.
17. 'G 8 Summit', *The Independent*, 5 July 2005, page 6.
18. 'Ill winds that whisper the collapse of civilisation', *The Sydney Morning Herald*, www.smh.com.au/articles/2005/09/231126982230-825.html> Tim Flannery, *The Weather Makers*, op. cit., pages 104-113.

Pastoral Letter on the Great Barrier Reef, written by the Catholic Bishops of Queensland in June 2004, when enumerating the problems facing that ecosystem speaks of the problems connected with climate change, particularly coral bleaching and rising sea levels.[19] If global warming continues at its present rate almost half the coral reefs could be lost within the next forty years.

Scientists in Antarctica have discovered that global warming and the rise in sea temperature is having a very negative impact on wildlife in that region of the world. Within a few decades the population levels of many creatures, including whales, seals and krill, could be affected. A study in 2005 found that the oceans to the west of the Antarctic peninsula had warmed by one degree since the 1960s. This was the first evidence that the southern ocean was getting warmer. The accepted theory until now was that ice, bitterly cold winds and currents would keep these waters cold and protect the creatures that live there.

Lloyd Peck, a marine biologist with the British Antarctic Survey, said that 'the sea temperature is going up in a way that wasn't predicted and this makes me more worried for the marine animals. The evidence we've got, and the models we've been looking at, said sea temperature was not likely to change much in Antarctica. A one degree increase puts us into the region where animals are pushed to one end of their biological, physiological and ecological capabilities … If the warming goes on at the same rate for 50 or 100 years then lots of populations of animals I work on, and maybe entire species, would be at risk.'[20]

One of the species most at risk is krill. A study published in 2004 found that krill numbers had decreased by 80% since 1970. Scientists link this near collapse of krill to shrinking sea ice. Krill are crustaceans that can grow up to 6 cm. They are the staple food

19. *Let the Many Coastlands be Glad*, (Ps 97), *Pastoral Letter on the Great Barrier Reef*, by The Catholic Bishops of Queensland, page 17.
20. David Adams, 'Sea ice melts and glaciers shrink at accelerating rate: Decline in stocks of krill hits entire food chain', *The Guardian*, 19 October 2005, page 9.

of many marine species, especially whales. A dramatic decline in krill could have catastrophic consequences for marine life.

About one half of all the extra carbon dioxide which humans have injected into the atmosphere during the past 200 years has ended up in the oceans. This carbon dioxide is making the oceans more acidic. It is estimated that there has been a change of 0.1 of a pH unit since the beginning of the industrial revolution. This may not seem to be a huge increase but it means that the upper layer of the ocean is 30% more acidic than it was in the year 1800.[21] The acidification of the oceans will affect the thousands of marine species which build their skeletons from calcium carbonate. These include mollusks, corals and other calcifying organisms. These are finding it difficult to grow their shells in the slightly more acidic water. One of the group of creatures affected in this way is the marine plant called colithophorids. This plant lies at the base of the marine food chain. A research team, led by Ulf Riebesel from the Alfred Wenger Institute for Polar and Marin Research in Germany, found that under the kind of acidic conditions which are developing in the upper oceans by the year 2100 coccolithophorid shell growth would be 83% slower than at present. This would have dire consequences for all the animals that, in one way or another, feed of these creatures.[22]

*Major Problems with Fresh Water*

Global Warming will affect the availability of fresh water for human consumption and for agriculture. On a global level, Northern winters are predicted to be wetter and summers drier. The monsoons in South and South East Asia will be much wetter but many areas like Southern Europe, Central America, Africa and Australia will be much drier.

An increase in rainfall in tropical environments may not be proved correct if the predictions of David Rind, of the Goddard

---

21. Thomas E. Lovejoy, 'Rising acidity threatens marine life', *International Herald-Tribune*, 7 June 2006, page 8.
22. Colin Woodward, 'Warming up the seas' *E The Environmental Magazine*, July / August 2005, page 39.

Institute for Space Studies in New York, are right. In chapter one, I discussed how over the years researchers at GISS have built up a sophisticated computer climate model. When Rind ran this model which factored in different amounts of carbon dioxise, he found that as carbon dioxide levels increase in the atmosphere the world experienced more fresh water shortages. These shortages began at the tropics and continued up to the poles. When it reached 500 ppm of carbon dioxide, which is the predicted level by 2050, vast areas of the US appeared to be suffering from severe drought.[23]

In Western Australia, for example, winter rainfall was reliable from the period when records began around 1829 up until 1975. This meant that farmers could plant winter wheat and be certain that the crop would get sufficient rain. However, since 1975 the average rainfall has fallen by 15%. Climatologists claim that much of this decline is due to global warming. This decrease in rainfall has had a catastrophic affect on wheat farming, driving many farmers from the land.

The city of Perth, which is the capital of Western Australia, has also suffering from a serious water problem. With the virtual disappearance of the winter rains, Perth has had to draw on underground water reserves called the Gnangara Mound. To offset the water loss the authorities began to mine this water. After thirty years, these reserves are at a critically low level. The water experts in Perth are very worried about the future. They have rated the chance of a 'catastrophic failure of supply' as 1 in 5. There are now plans to build a $350 million desalination plant to supply fresh water for the city. Even with this huge expenditure the plant will only supply 15% of the city's current water needs. So the future of this city of one and a half million people is very much in the balance and the main culprit is global warming.

Sydney, which is located on the East Coast of Australia, has much greater water storage capacity than Perth but droughts have plagued the city during the past decade and the future

23. Elizabeth Rolbert, 'Climate of Man- 11', *The New Yorker*, 2 May 2005, page 70.

looks bleak if temperatures rise as a result of global warming.[24] Capacity at Warragamba Dam, which supplies about 80% of Sydney's water, is down to 37.2%. It is estimated that at the present consumption levels, Sydney will face a 200 billion litre water shortage by the year 2030. It is ironic that Australians, who live on the driest inhabited continent on earth, are among the world's highest water users. Solving their problems with fresh water is going to be costly. It will involve stricter conservation measures, water charges and massive expenditure on desalination plants.[25]

Higher temperatures will mean greater water loss due to evaporation. The combined effects of less rain and more evaporation will have a very negative impact on the possibility of growing different kinds of crops on various soil types. Areas of the world like the Philippines, where rice is grown in paddy fields, may no longer have sufficient water for that pattern of cropping. The elaborate and expensive irrigation systems which were built in the Philippines during the second part of the 20th century may become redundant.

In January 2006, approximately 11 million people faced starvation in Ethiopia, Kenya, Somalia and Djibouti because of lack of rain. Klaus Toepfer, of the United Nations Environment Agency, is convinced that climate change is one of the reasons for the drought. He also includes deforestation as a cause of the drought. This reduces the ability of the land to make the most out of the rains when they come.[26] On a global level, according to Oxfam, over 3 billion people in the Middle East and the Indian

24. Tim Flannery, *The Climate Makers*, Allen Lane, Penguin, pages 103-131.
25. Xenya Cheerny, 'Drought-hit-Sydney Tackles Water Crisis', Reuter News Service, Australia, 8 May 2005. www.planetark.com/daily-newsstory.cfm/newsid/30713/story.htm
26. Rob Crilly, 'Climate change a matter of life and death in Africa', *The Irish Times*, 14 January 2006, page 11.

sub-continent and elsewhere could be facing acute shortages of water.[27]

As the temperature increases, global warming models predict that in Ireland there will be an increase in water runoffs from the land during the wet winter months in the western and north western parts of the country. This will give rise to increased flooding. In contrast, there will be much less rain in the eastern part of Ireland especially during the summer months. It is estimated that rainfall could be down by 30%.[28] Given that the majority of people of Ireland live in Leinster, especially around the Dublin area, it may be necessary to pipe water from Lough Ree in the midlands to meet the capital's water needs. Farmers on the east coast of Ireland may also have to consider irrigating their crops and even abandoning particular kinds of crops which have been grown traditionally for centuries in Ireland, as we will see later.

*Desertification*

Deserts make up about 25% of the earth's land surface and roughly 500 million people live in them. Scientists believe that desertification is being exacerbated by global warming. Climate change is making many semi-arid regions of the world drier. With temperatures increasing as well as a lack of available clean water, life will become more and more unbearable for many of the 500 million people who are living in deserts. Cities such as Riyadh in Saudi Arabia and Phoenix in the US may not have a very promising future as their water tables drop and become more salty.

It is obvious that deserts are spreading: over 770 square miles of China becomes desert each year. One cannot argue that global warming is the only cause of this phenomenon as over grazing

27. 'World governments fail to act on aid as water crisis worsens' press release; 19 April 2004, www.oxfam.org.uk/press/release/watercrisis-190404.hlm
28. John Sweeney, et al., *Climate Change: Scenarios and Impacts for Ireland*, Enviropnmental Protection Agency, PO Box 3000, Johnstown Castle, Co Wexford, page 98.

and other destructive agricultural practices also take their toll. Nevertheless, global warming does play a significant role and the situation is getting worse. Long-term weather records indicate that there is declining rainfall as well as increasing temperatures in recent decades.[29] Desertification in some marginal and dry lands in China and many other areas of the world will be increased because of the vicious cycle of more intense droughts which are predicted to follow in the wake of global warming during the 21st century.

The Dashti Kbir desert in Iran has seen a 16% drop in rainfall patterns in the past 15 years. In the Kalahari desert in Africa rainfall is down by 12% and in the Atacama desert in Chile it has dropped 8%.[30] Droughts are also affecting Pakistan. On 7 May 2006 the newspaper *Dawn* carried a report from the meteorological department warning of a possible drought in the country, with no significant rainfall expected during the following two months. The drought is expected to be particularly evident in the Sindh and Baluchistan provinces. It is expected to hit crop production and around one million people.[31]

A report published by *World Wide Fund for Nature* in January 2003, argued that global warming was responsible for record day time temperatures in Australia in 2002 and caused an unprecedented rate of water evaporation all over the dry continent. This process is contributing to increased desertification. The report was endorsed by researchers at the government-funded Commonwealth Scientific and Industrial Research Organisation (CSIRO). Kevin Hennessy, a senior researcher at CSIRO's Atmospheric Research Department, predicted that the Murray-Darling Basin, which covers almost the whole of inland South East Australia, would get between a half a degree and two degrees celsius warmer by 2030 and ten percent drier.[32] It is inter-

29. David Adams, op.cit., page 9.
30. John Vidal, 'Deserts cities are living on borrowed time, UN warns', *The Guardian*, 5 June 2006. www.guardian.co.uk/print),,329496810-110970,00, html 05/06/2006>
31. Sher Baz Khan, 'Pakistan facing drought threat', *Dawn*, 8 May 2006.
32. www.planetark.com/dailynewsstory.html

CHAPTER THREE 45

esting to note that Australia, with carbon-dioxide emissions of 27.6 tonnes per person annually, is the highest in the world. This is mainly because of the fact that most of its power comes from coal-burning power plants. Australia exports much of its coal to other Asian countries, especially Japan. This is why the government led by Prime Minister John Howard has failed to ratify the Kyoto Protocol. While looking at these carbon dioxide league tables, the United States and Canada follow closely in the wake of Australia with Ireland taking up fourth place. While India and China have expanded their economies in recent years, the US emissions per person is 6 times greater than those of China and 13 times greater than those of India.[33]

Until very recently, much of the concerns about human-induced climate change focused on the polar regions. New satellite data seems to be indicating that the tropical zones of the world are also affected and are expanding because of global warming. This new data, which is based on measurements taken from satellites over 25 years, show that the tropics have widened by 140 miles since 1979. Based on this data in 2006, Professor Thomas Reicher in the US stated that this expansion of the tropics is taking place in both hemispheres. What Professor Reicher and his colleagues at the University of Washington, as well as researchers at Lanzhou University in China, found is that the major warm air stream, sometimes called 'the jet stream', which flows through the atmosphere at 30,000 to 50,000 feet, has moved one degree both north and south.

According to Professor John Wallace, these jet streams mark the edge of the tropics. So, if they are moving poleward, that means the tropics are getting wider. This is very worrying because it is in the area immediately outside the tropics that most of the world's deserts are situated. These also seem to be moving towards the Arctic and Antarctic. This may be the explanation

33. Just Comment: a joint publication of the Edmund Rice Centre for Justice and Community Education and The School of Education Catholic University, Vol 4, 2005, page 1. Data from Comprehensive emissions per capita for industrialised countries, Hal Turton and Clive Hamilton, The Australian Institute, 2001.

for the fact that in recent times there has been a prolonged drought in southern Europe and in the south-western US. Many heavily populated areas are affected by prolonged droughts from China through North India on to the Middle East, North Africa, Florida, the US Gulf Coast, South Africa, Argentina and Australia.[34] There is reason to believe that droughts in the western part of the US might be a more permanent feature of life in that part of the world. The mighty Colorado river is only a shadow of its former self. Kevin Trenberth, of the National Center for Atmospheric Research in Boulder, Colorado, has called attention to the fact that the percentage of the world's land area affected by serious drought has doubled in the past 30 years. In the 1970s, only 15% of land was drought-stricken. In 2006, it had reached 30%.[35]

*Climate Change will increase Health Problems*
Climate change has an impact on human physical health in a number of different ways. Details of some of these impacts can be found in a carefully researched paper by the World Health Organisation. Some of the details of this paper were contained in a report published in the journal *Nature* in November 2005. It stated that the world's poorest countries face a dramatic increase in deaths from diseases such as malaria, dengue fever, diarrhorea and malnutrition as a direct result of climate change.[36] Severe flooding can cause the discharge of sewage into drinking water thus spreading waterborne diseases. These conditions are also favourable for an outbreak of cholera.

The World Health Organisation (WHO) has estimated that the earth's hotter climate will contribute to more than 150,000 deaths and 5 million illnesses each year. This figure could dou-

---

34. Geoffry Lean, 'Widening tropics will drive deserts into Europe' *The Independent*, 4 June 2006. www.independent.co.uk/environment-news/04/06/2006>
35. 'Why deserts will inherit the Earth' www.new.independent. co.uk/environment/article25034.ece/05/06/2006 page 5, from Fred Pearce, The Last Generation, Transworld, London, 2006.
36. Ian Sampie, 'Climate change will fuel disease among poor', *The Sydney Morning Herald*, 18 November 2005, page 4.

ble by the year 2030. Health and climate scientists at the University of Wisconsin in Madision have conducted the most comprehensive studies to date to measure global warming. They have said that rising temperatures will have a dispropor-tionate effect on poor countries. These poor countries have done little to create the problem in the first place. According to the sci-entist, Jonathan Patz who led the study at the university's Gaylord Nelson Institute for Environmental Studies and its Department of Population Health Sciences, the regions most at risk from climate changes include the Asian and South American Pacific coasts, the Indian Ocean coast and sub-Saharan Africa.[37]

But even in Europe and the US, the effect of climate change is already evident. The 2003 heat wave in Europe resulted in a death toll of 30,000 above the normal level of deaths at that time of year for a two week period. Many of those who died were el-derly people. Extreme heat can also affect young children and those who are suffering from heart disease, strokes or breathing problems. During the summer of 1999, which was considered to be the hottest and driest for over a century, 62 people became ill with West Nile encephalitis. This disease causes inflammation of the brain and can be very serious. Seven people died as result of it in the US in 1999. This was the first time this disease was re-ported in New York. The disease is spread by a mosquito called *culex pipens* which breeds in stagnant water. Under normal cir-cumstance this mosquito attacks birds but during a drought birds may not be available because they have flown off in search of fresh water. With few of its normal potential hosts around, the mosquito attacks people instead.[38] Dr Paul Epstein of Harvard University has also highlighted the connection between global warming and West Nile encephalitis. By 2002, West Nile en-cephalitis had spread across the US and was found in 44 states as well as in Washington, DC.

---

37. ibid.
38. Jim Motavalli, 'Feeling the Heat; The World Warms Up'. *Our Planet*, newsletter1@emagazine, week of 26 March 2006.

According to Dr Dickson Despommier, a professor of public health at Columbia University, higher temperatures also trigger increased mosquito biting frequency. He also sees a similar pattern of events and new colonisation by the mosquito in places as far apart as Romania, South Africa and Israel. A fact sheet prepared jointly, in September 2005, by the Australia Medical Association and the Australia Conservation Foundation addressed some of the health concerns associated with climate change. They claimed that even with the mild change in temperature between the mid 1970s and the end of the century, 250,000 people had died as a result of climate change. It also warned that in Australia, temperature deaths could rise by 2,500 per annum by 2020. Also flood-related deaths and injuries may increase by 240% in some regions. Warmer temperatures and more variable rainfall will increase the intensity and frequency of food-borne and water-borne diseases.

*Global Warming and Extinction*

In January 2004, Dr Chris Thomas of Leeds University in Britain published an article in the magazine *Nature* on the impact of climate change on the natural world. He and his team of scientists from around the world estimated that, over the next 50 years, climate change is expected to drive one quarter of land animals and plants over the precipice of extinction. The paper was based on two years of research. According to Dr Thomas, 'when the scientists set about the research they hoped to come up with definite results, but what we found we wished we had not. It is far worse than we thought, and what we have discovered may be an underestimation.[39]

Quite a significant proportion of this extinction spasm is being caused by changes in local temperatures. As the climate changes some species will not be able to adapt quickly enough to the changes and will simply become extinct. In Australia, up to 54% of the continent's butterfly species could become extinct

---

39. Paul Brown, 'An unnatural disaster', *The Guardian*, 8 January 2004, page 1.

before 2050. Orange Whitespot Skipper (*Trapezites heteromacula*) and Western Jewel butterflies (*Hypochrysops halyaetus*) face losing 90% to 98% of their distribution range due to climate change. Boyd's Forest Dragon (*Hypsilurus boydi*) is especially vulnerable. Worse still a 25% extinction rate for European birds has been predicted.[40]

Frogs and amphibians are particularly vulnerable to extinction. There are about 5,743 species of amphibians in the world. According to recent research 32.5% are threatened with extinction. The environmental changes brought about by climate change are contributing to their destruction.[41]

The zoologist Tim Flannery gives a good example of how global warming is causing extinction. The only food that caterpillar of the winter moth (*Operopthera brumata*) will eat are the leaves of young oak trees. Because of global warming, this winter moth now hatches three weeks earlier than it did fifty years ago. Unfortunately, the oak leaves on which it depends may not appear until three weeks after the moth hatches. Since the caterpillars can only survive for a few days without the appropriate food, there are now much fewer winter moths and the species as a whole could be facing extinction.[42]

It is difficult to say how much Irish flora and fauna will be affected by climate change. The authors of *Climate Change: Scenarios and Impacts in Ireland* are aware that there is a huge lack of baseline data on biodiversity in Ireland. This makes predictions with regard to what might happen difficult. There is agreement that the aquatic environment of the Arctic char (*Salvelinus alpinus*) and smelt (*Osmerus eperlanus*) will come under stress. The coastal areas which will be affected by climate change are very important for migratory birds, especially waders. Species that might win out by extending their base include the natterjack toad (*Bufo calamita*) and the lesser horseshoe bat (*Rhinlofus hipposideros*). In contrast to their cousins in Australia, insect

40. John von Radowitz, *Irish Examiner*, 1 September 2004, page 3.
41. Ian Sample, 'Disease, habitat loss and climate change threatens amphibians', *The Guardian*, 7 July 2006, page 13.
42. Tim Flannery, *Weather Makers*, op. cit., page 89 -90.

species, especially butterflies, should do well but some more predatory insects may not be to our liking, such as malaria-bearing mosquitos. In the area of plants, introduced species like montbretia and rhododendron will probably thrive.

In the marine environment changes in sea levels will lead to a significant loss in estuarine habitat. Species may not be able to migrate because of human or natural obstacles and therefore will suffer what is called coastal 'squeeze'.[43] Warmer seas may attract more mullet, bass, red gurnard and even tuna.

*Impact on Forests*

Forests, especially tropical rainforests, stabilise global climate by locking up billions of tons of carbon in their vegetation. It is estimated that a typical tree absorbs a tonne of carbon for every cubic metre of growth.[44] Destruction of forests is one of the major causes of global warming. When forests are destroyed, they release millions of tonnes of carbon dioxide into the atmosphere.

Forests will also come under stress from global warming. Different species of trees grow in areas which are suitable for their development. In the natural course of evolutionary events which happen over thousands of years, forest ecosystems, when confronted with ecological stress, can adapt to the new situation by moving further north or south. This will not be possible with global warming because of the speed at which climate change is happening. Trees, which are already diseased, will be subject to stress and therefore vulnerable to attack by other diseases or pests. Even at this point in the cycle of change, studies of trees in different parts of Canada have found that disease and die-back is not the result of acid rain but rather is attributable to a succession of warmer winters and drier summers.[45]

Forestry is one area where global warming could benefit Ireland. At present we have one of the lowest rate of tree cover

43. John Sweeney et al., *Climate Change: Scenarios and Impact for Ireland*, EPA, 2003, page 227.
44. David Hickey, 'Nature's Corridors', *The Irish Times*, 8 February 2005.
45. John Haughton, *Global Warming*, op.cit., page 173.

in Europe at 9% of the land area of the country. An increase in carbon dioxide levels will stimulate tree growth.[46] However, what you gain on the 'swings' you lose on the 'roundabouts', because the increase of storms and winter rain due to global warming could have a negative impact on forest yield.

## Impact on Agriculture

There are some archeologists who suspect that a shift in the earth's axis some 12,000 years ago was the impetus that gave rise to farming in the first instance. These same archeologists wonder whether the temperature changes taking place today might signal the end of agriculture as we know it. In the Andes in South America, there is a discernible change in climate – the weather is much wetter. This is having a detrimental effect on potato cultivation. The wetter climate creates the conditions for blight to move 4,000 feet up into the mountains where it was never found before. In 2003 almost the whole crop of native potatoes was destroyed by blight.[47]

In Asia the effect of climate change is being felt by rice and wheat farmers. Again it is linked to the availability of rain at the proper time. Lack of rain affects poor farmers most of all because they seldom have access to irrigation. Such farmers rely almost totally on the annual monsoons for irrigation. But these monsoons have been less reliable in recent years, partly, it is thought because of the El Niño effect. (This refers to the cyclical pattern of heat on surface water in the eastern Pacific, mainly off the coast of Peru. In the past it usually happened around Christmas time which is why it is called El Niño after the Christ Child.) Many predict that with climate change El Niño events will increase in the future. I remember the devastation which the 1983 El Niño event caused in Mindanao in the Philippines, especially among tribal people called the T'boli people who lived in the mountains. They were reduced to eating banana leaves to survive.

46. John Sweeney et al, *Climate Change: Scenarios and Impacts for Ireland*, EPA, page 225.
47 Brian Halweil, 'The Irony of Climate', *World-Watch*, March/April, 2005, pp 18 -23.

The drought caused severe loss of crops in Indonesia. Non-irrigated maize was down 55% and even the irrigated crops were down 41%. The irrigated rice crop was down 34%, and the cassava crop was down 19%. The fear among the farmers and agriculturalists is that this trend will continue under a regime of global warming. David Rind, who is a senior climate researcher with NASA's Goddard Institute for Space Studies, is on record as saying that, 'if we get a substantial global warming, there is no doubt in my mind that there will be serious changes to the monsoons'.[48] This is the nub of the problem because it is the rainfall patterns which are at the foundation of successful agriculture in almost every part of the world. There is evidence that the rainfall patterns from the plains of northern China to southern Africa and south east Asia are changing in unpredictable ways, often bringing prolonged droughts which are detrimental to agriculture.

There is also the concern about how plants will react to significantly higher temperatures. Hartwell Allen works as a researcher with the US Department of Agriculture and the University of Florida. For over 20 years he has been experimenting with growing plants at different temperatures and with different atmospheric carbon dioxide content. His findings are worthy of note. When he doubled the carbon dioxide content in the atmosphere and raised the temperature slightly, the plants and tubers grew higher and bigger. But once the temperature was raised significantly higher, things began to deteriorate. Every part of the growing process was damaged significantly.[49]

John Sheedy, a biologist at the International Rice Research in Los Banos near Manila, found that damage to rice happens if the temperature exceeds 30 degrees celsius during the flowering period. At 40 degrees celsius there is no yield at all. He is convinced that rice, wheat and maize yields will drop by 10% for every 1 degree celsius rise in temperature. It is the higher temperatures during the night which do most of the damage. This is

48. Ibid, page 18, 19.
49. Ibid, page 19.

because the plants have to work harder to respire and this saps their energy thus lowering the yield. If current climate change predictions continue, cereal yields in tropical countries could drop by up to 30% during the next 50 years. This would certainly increase the number of poor, hungry people in many countries, especially as populations increase.

The economy of China has grown spectacularly for the past decade and a half. Though there is wide disparity in income, especially between urban and remote rural areas, there is not nearly the same level of devastating poverty and hunger as was there in past. Nevertheless, providing food for over 1.3 billion people will demand millions of tonnes of food in the future, particularly if global warming lowers the yield of key staple crops like rice and wheat.

In fact, climate change could derail China's recently achieved food security. A study jointly organised by the governments of China and the United Kingdom found that China's yields of rice, wheat and maze could drop between 20% and 37% if the most serious predictions of the scientists with regard to global warming proved correct. Though crops generally grow faster in the presence of high levels of carbon dioxide in the atmosphere, that benefit can be offset by variability in precipitation levels and soil nutrition. Further complicating the agricultural picture in China would be the possibilities of increased disease and pest infestations which are known to migrate into new territory with warming climates. The study also found that China is likely to experience more extreme climatic effects including hotter summers and more intense rainfalls. Average temperatures across China will likely rise between 3 and 4 degrees celsius by the end of 21st century. Large proportions of China's population could slip back into hunger and poverty, based on the study's projections.

To summarise, climate change will bring an increase in severe weather conditions. There will be increased amounts of rain and wind as well as weather extremes ranging from flood to droughts. This is not good news for most of the stable foods of the world. For a few thousand years farmers grew staple crops in virtually stable climatic conditions. With global warming farmers will have to plant a wider variety of crops than they did in the recent past in order to safeguard themselves and their produce. This, in fact, could be a good thing because the present monocropping system of agriculture, which is found in both temperate and tropical regions, is not sustainable in the long run. It depletes the soil of nutrients, causes massive erosion and is dependent on diminishing fossil fuel supplies.

In many parts of the world, farmers are already involved in agroforestry. This involves planting crops like cereals and root crops between fruit trees and other kinds of trees. This three-dimension agriculture, with crops growing beneath the soil, on the soil and on the trees, can protect cereal crops against the heat and secure the soils against wind erosion. The tree roots will help retain moisture in the soil, making it more available to the crops. It also improves humus in the soil.

As global warming increases and fossil fuels become more expensive and difficult to obtain, local production of food will become much more economically viable. It will no longer make economic sense to haul basic foods stuffs half way around the world when transport cost are factored into the equation.

Experts do not believe that climate change will have a more catastrophic impact on agriculture in Ireland than it will have in other areas. Still there could be significant changes. Cereal crops like barley might succumb to blight because of rising tempera-tures and damp autumns. The crop that will benefit most is maize. The yields should be up significantly so that its use as a high-energy, fodder crop will be enhanced. With an increase in temperature and less summer rain, farmers might turn to grow-ing soybeans. The big loser is likely to be the traditional humble potato. Less summer rain may mean that its successful cultiv-ation will depend on installing expensive irrigation systems.

Rearing livestock on the farm of the future will depend on the changing patterns of grass production. This should improve and the mild winters should lessen the time that the animals have to stay indoors. Unfortunately, even though the weather would be milder, the extra rain may inhibit the farmer from putting the animals out doors because of water-logged pastures.[50]

Animal husbandry will probably have to come to terms with belching and flatulence from cows, sheep and other ruminants. This accounts for about 15% of methane emissions worldwide. With over 6 million cattle in Ireland, and even more sheep, this is a significant concern in the overall strategy of controlling greenhouse gas emissions. The problem is that methane is a highly polluting greenhouse gas. Researchers in Scotland have developed a feed additive which reduces flatulence and belching in ruminants. The feed additive contains fumaric acid which means that the hydrogen, which is one of the elements contained in the methane molecule, is metabolically trapped in the cow. John Wallace, a researcher at the Rowett Research Institute in Scotland where this feed is being developed, explains the process. 'Methane is a high-energy fuel – we use it in domestic cooking. When methane formation is inhibited, you can imagine that the energy is retained in the animal rather than being lost to the atmosphere.' This feed supplement could deliver a benefit both to the farmer, as the animals will put on more weight, and to the environment, with less methane emissions.[51]

*People and Cultures Under Threat*

Climate change will also threaten to wipe out many cultures. For example, higher temperatures in the Arctic is endangering the culture and livelihood of the Inuit people living in remote Arctic villages in Northern Canada, US and Russia. The animals on which they depend, especially seals and caribou, are no longer plentiful in their environment. Climate change has been evident to them for the past twenty years. In the past there were at least five months of snow and the temperature was cold enough to

---

50. John Sweeney, 2003, *Climate Change Scenarios and Impacts for Ireland*, EPA, page 224.
51. Dr Marina Murphy, 'New diet to curb bovine emissions', *The Irish Times*, 9 February 2006, page 15.

enable them to build their igloos. Now there is only six weeks of constant snow for them to build their igloos. The change in climate is also altering their ability to hunt for food as the traditional season for the arrival of either the caribou or the beluga whales has changed. Caribou have starved to death because of lack of vegetation in their tundra area. In the past three decades 400,000 square miles of sea ice has melted. The ice is now also 40% thinner which has a devastating impact on the nomadic way of life of the Inuit people. The weather is also very unpredictable. This means that when they go hunting they use a tent instead of the traditional igloo. But if the temperature drops too low they might very well freeze to death.[52] They are no longer nomadic at this point in their history and, given the speed of climate change, they appear to be one of the first societies who will fall victim to global warming.

All the changes have had a huge impact on their lives. In many instances it has lead to both alcohol and drug abuse. Teenage suicide rates are among the highest in the world. In a petition to the Inter Commission on Human Rights, Inuit people describe many accidents which have happened as a result of the warming of the area. Lizzie Gordon, who lives on the east coast near Nunavik, the capital of Kuijjuak, described losing several members of her family in a freak blizzard. Even experienced hunters are falling through thin ice. Sometimes these accidents are fatal. Often it is too dangerous to drive a skidoo.[53]

Island communities, especially in the Pacific area, are also in great danger from rising seas. During high tide in Kiribati many of the houses are flooded and the fresh water sources are being contaminated. One hundred villagers from Lateu, in northern Vanuatu in the Pacific, have been relocated on higher ground after their coastal homes where repeatedly swamped by storm

52. Clare Kendall, 'Life on the Edge of a Warming World', *The Ecologist*, July-August 2006, pages 026-028.
53. Clare Kendall, 'Climate forces Inuit onto thin ice', *Sydney Morning Herald*, 27 May 2006. www.smh.com.au/articles/2006/05/26/114852 4886121.htmal, pages 1 and 2.

surges and aggressive waves linked with climate change. Over recent years the rate of flooding has increased, triggering a variety of problems including increased incidences of malaria and skin diseases among children. The UN Environment Programme (UNEP) is developing national adaptation programmes in more than a dozen countries that are vulnerable to climate change.[54]

---

54. www.climateimc.org/?g=no de/183

# CHAPTER 4

# Responses to Climate Change

*Denial*

Within a few months of being elected president, George W. Bush repudiated the Kyoto Protocol. This was in part due to pressure from Exxon-Mobil, the world's most powerful oil company. In documentation that became available before the G8 meeting in Gleneagle, Scotland in June 2005, briefing papers from the Bush administration repeatedly thanked Exxon Mobile executives for helping them shape their policies on climate change. In 2003, Nick Thomas, Exxon's head of public affairs, denied such involvement in a submission given to the UK's House of Lords Science and Technology Committee. The documentation obtained by Greenpeace under the freedom of information legislation challenges Nick Thomas's version of events.[1]

Another reason why conservative groups and the Bush administration opposed Kyoto is that they claimed it would be an enormous financial burden, which would slow down the US economy and as a consequence jobs would be exported overseas to nations that had not signed up to the Kyoto agreement. The US Department of Energy claimed that the cut-backs under Kyoto would cost $378 billion annually. This was disputed by the Clinton administration. According to their calculations, the bill would be in the region of $1 billion annually. Other commentators, like William Nordhaus of Yale University and his colleague Dale Jorgenson of Harvard University, predict that the cost of complying with Kyoto would be quite modest and would not bankrupt the country as conservative groups were claiming. The cost of complying with Kyoto must be off-set

---

1. John Vidal, 'Revealed: how oil giant influenced Bush', *The Guardian*, 8 June 2005, page 4.

against the cost of doing nothing and thereby paying the price for more devastating hurricanes than those experienced in 2005. These will cost tens of billions of dollars. If one included the effect of heat waves and other climatic events, which we now know are caused by global warming, the cost rises even further.

Returning to the current political sphere in the US, there is also solid evidence that officials in the Bush administration altered serious scientific reports that linked greenhouse gases with global warming. Philip Cooney, chief of staff of the White House Council on Environmental Quality, was involved in such distortions even though he lacked any significant scientific training. He deleted a paragraph which stated that 'melting glaciers would change flood patterns and threaten native populations', with the dismissive comment that the assertions were, 'straying from research into speculative findings/musings'.[3] The most shocking revelation about Mr Cooney is that before coming to the White House he had been a senior lobbyist for the American Petroleum Institute. This is the largest trade group which represents the oil industry.[4] This group has consistently claimed that the uncertainties involved in the global warming debate justify the delay in restricting greenhouse gas emissions.[5]

Many of the conservative and free market 'think-tanks', like the Cato Institute in the US, have opposed the Kyoto Protocol. Among those funding Cato are many of the big oil companies like Exxon-Mobile, Chevron Texaco and Tenneco. Cato has published reports questioning the scientific basis for global warming. Among these publications are *Climate of Fear: Why We Shouldn't Worry About Global Warming*, and *Meltdown: The Predictable Distortion of Global Warming by Scientists, Politicians and the Media*.[6]

2. Tim Flannery, *The Weather Makers*, op. cit., pages 233 - 236.
3. Roland Watson , 'Bush aide altered climate reports', *The Times* (World News), 9 June 2005, page 39.
4. Andrew C. Revkin, 'Bush Aide Softened Greenhouse Gas Links to Global Warming', *The New York Times*, 8 June 2005. www.netimes.com/2005/96/08poltics
5. ibid. page 2 of 3.
6. David Cromwell, 'Burning the Planet for Profit,' *Znet Commentary* 18 January 2006. www.zmag.org/sustainers/content/14/01/ 2006 cromwell.cfm

Senator James Inhofe, chairman of the powerful Committee on Environment and Public Works, described global warming as the greatest hoax ever perpetrated on the American people.[7]

Lobby groups funded by the oil industry are not only active in the US. Bob May, president of the Royal Society, warned that such groups were targeting Britain in order to get politicians to play down the threat of global warming and climate change. His warning came just as a group called Scientific Alliance was scheduling a meeting of climate change skeptics in London in January 2005. In December 2004, this group published a joint Report, in conjunction with the George C Marshall Institute in Washington, which they claimed undermined the data which the majority of climate change scientists used to prove that global warming is happening.

Coincidently at the same time a group of British scientists published their research in the journal *Nature* showing that the greenhouse effect could have a more devastating impact on climate even if levels of greenhouse gases are kept below 500 ppm by 2050. They claim that the average temperature could rise by 11 degrees celsius. The person who co-ordinated the research, David Frame, said that 'If the real world response were anywhere near the upper end of our range, even today's levels of greenhouse gases could already be dangerously high.'[8]

There is no doubt about the fact that the hurricane season of 2005, especially hurricane Katrina, began to change public opinion in the US with regard to climate change. The increase in oil prices has also heightened awareness about the future. For this reason President Bush devoted a short section, two minutes and 15 seconds to be precise, of his 2006 State of the Union address to energy issues. He said that the US needed to abandon its 'addiction' to imported oil. In order to reverse this dangerous trend he has set about trying to replace 75% of the country's oil imports from the Middle East with biofuels by 2025.

7. Jim Hansen, 'The Threat to the Planet', *The New York Review*, 13 July 2006, page 14.
8. David Adam, 'Oil firms fund campaign to deny climate change', *The Guardian*, 27 January 2005, page 1.

The editorial in *The New York Times* the following day dismissed these remarks as woefully insufficient. Later on, the editorial addressed President Bush's unwillingness to confront global warming: 'Of all the defects in Mr Bush's energy presentation, the greatest was his unwillingness to address global warming – an energy-related emergency every bit as critical as our reliance on foreign oil. Except for a few academics on retainer at the more backward energy companies, virtually no educated scientist disputes that the earth has grown warmer over the last few decades – largely as a result of increasing atmospheric concentrations of carbon dioxide produced by burning fossil fuels.' The editorial ended by reflecting on the true scale of President Bush's negligence in not confronting global warming: 'That Mr Bush has taken a pass on this issue is a negligence from which the globe may never recover. While he seems finally to have signed on to the idea that the earth is warming, and that humans are heavily responsible, he has rejected serious proposals to do anything about it and allowed his advisers on the issue to engage in a calculated program of disinformation. At the recent global summit on warming, his chief spokesman insisted that the president's program of voluntary reductions by individual companies has resulted in a reduction in emissions, when in fact the reverse is true.'[9]

It is worth noting that the President's promise to break his country's addiction to oil received a better press in London. They were particularly pleased with his proposal to make cellulosic ethanol derived from agricultural waste a competitive and practical fuel for cars within six years. There are at present 220 million cars in the US and only 2% of the transport fuel is bioethanol. There is some irony in the fact that within a week of these new pledges the Energy Department laid off staff at the National Renewable Energy Laboratory near Denver because of budget cuts. These dropped from $202 million to $174 million in

---

9. Editorial, 'The State of Energy', *The New York Times*, February 1, 2006. www.nytimes.com/2006/02/01>

62                                    CLIMATE CHANGE

2005. The cuts are for the fiscal year that began on October 1, 2005. Forty staff members out of a total of 930 are to lose their jobs.[10]

*David Bellamy*

Another person who has downplayed global warming is the well-known botanist, David Bellamy. In a letter to the *New Scientist* (16 April 2005) he wrote that glaciers around the world 'are not shrinking but in fact are growing'. He claimed that '555 of all the 625 glacier under observation by the World Glacier Monitoring Service (WGMS) in Zurich, Switzerland have grown since 1980'.[11] George Monbiot phoned the organisation which Bellamy quoted and they repudiated Bellamy's contention. The spokesperson for the WGMS stated that the data which Bellamy was quoting was simply false, that it failed to provide any credible references and it overlooked both the scientific context and the current scientific literature on the subject.

When challenged by Monbiot, Bellamy called attention to a website www.iceagenow.com This website is the creation of Robert W. Felix who believes that, instead of having to worry about global warming, we are heading towards an ice age. Data resembling what Bellamy quoted in his letter to the *NewScientist* are on this website. Ultimately, Monbiot traced the data back to Professor Fred Singer who posted them on his website www.sepp.org But where did he get the figures? The research trail ended in a paper published in *Science* in 1989. Monbiot checked all the editions of *Science* published in 1989 and found no reference to data on shrinking glaciers. So Bellamy's claims have no basis in data. Anyone who lives near glaciers in any part of the world and has watched them for the past 30 years knows that, with a few exceptions, glaciers are retreating, and in some instances at an extraordinary rate.

10. Elizabeth Bumiller, 'Bush's Goals on Energy Quickly Find Obstacles', *The New York Times*, 2 February 2006. www.nytimes.com/ 2006/02/02/politics/02energy.html?
11. George Monbiot, 'Junk Science', *The Guardian*, 10 May 2005. www. Monbiot.com/archives/2005/05/10/junk science/page 1 of 4.

*Bjorn Lomborg*

The well-known Danish mathematician, Bjorn Lomborg, does not deny that global warming is happening. He believes that it would cost too much to cut carbon dioxide emissions and that it would be better to spend money ensuring clean drinking water and sanitation, better health care facilities and education for all. He would target alleviating human suffering, especially AIDS in Africa rather than spending money on reducing fossil fuel emissions. Lomborg has assembled a group of economists, called the Copenhagen Consensus, who share his view that the cost of stabilising global temperatures exceeds the benefits.[12] This group estimates that tackling global warming within the terms of the Kyoto Protocol would cost at least £87 billion per annum.

In February 2006, the Royal Society in Britain took a stand against Lomborg. They argued that conventional economics are not capable of assessing the long-term adverse impact on human or planetary well-being of something as enormous as global warming. Any form of economics, from simple barter to our contemporary market economies, depends on a stable climate and environment. If, for example, global warming leads to continuous droughts then any form of human activity may well be precluded.

*Positive Responses to Climate Change*

Changing a significant proportion of the transport fleet to ethanol would reduce US greenhouse gas emissions by 15% according to a study published in the US journal *Science*.[13] There were, however, some reservations that the sums of money involved in promoting alternative fuels are miniscule; a mere $59 million in funding for new ethanol technology and $54 million for clean coal technology. Critics also point out that since coming into office President Bush has consistently opposed any

---

12. Bjorn Lomborg, 'Global Warming should not be our No 1 priority', *The Scotsman*, 1 December 2005, page 32.
13. Julian Borger, 'Bush hits the road to take a green message to his nation of oil addicts', *The Guardian*, 2 February 2006. www.guardian.co.uk/print/02022006. Pages 1 and 2.

plans to demand high fuel efficiency from car makers. It is important to recognise that many groups of people in the US, especially in the scientific community, never supported and still do not support President Bush's policies.

The National Academy of Sciences undertook a rigorous study of global warming as far back as 1979. The preliminary results were so shocking for President Jimmy Carter that he appointed an Ad Hoc Study Group on Carbon Dioxide and Climate. The group is often referred to as the Charney panel after the distinguished meteorologist Julie Charney, from the Massachusetts Institute of Technology, who chaired the panel. Their findings were unambiguous. The panel looked for any flaws in the work of scientists who were using computer models to predict significant warming due to human induced factors. They stated that 'if carbon dioxide continues to increase, the study group finds no reason to doubt that climate change will result and no reason to believe that these changes will be negligible'.[14] The study went on to state that if there is a doubling of carbon dioxide levels from the pre-industrial period this is likely to give rise to a global average temperature change of between plus 2.5 to 8 degrees Fahrenheit. They were also insistent on the fact that the wait-and-see approach which was adopted by successive US administrations from President Reagan to President George W. Bush would be the riskiest possible strategy because there may not be severe warning until carbon dioxide levels have reached such a point that climate change is inevitable. In the intervening years, hundreds of reports have been issued by scientific bodies in the US warning about climate change. The National Academy of Science issued almost 200 reports on global warming, but those in the administration who perceive that any action on climate change might undermine their short-term financial well-being called many of these reports 'junk-science'.

---

14. Elizabeth Kolbert, 'The Climate of Man – 1, *The New Yorker*, 25 April 2005, page 58.

Jim Hansen, the Director of the NASA Goddard Institute for Space Studies, makes an interesting point when he writes that 'the press and television, despite overwhelming scientific consensus concerning global warming, give equal time to fringe 'contrarians' supported by the fossil fuel industry'.[15]

Before the meeting of the G8 in Gleneagles in Scotland in June 2005, the US Academy of Sciences joined with other Science Academies from the G8 countries in a statement on global warming. It read, 'there is now strong evidence that significant global warming is occurring. It is likely that most of the warming in recent decades can be attributed to human activities ... The scientific understanding of climate change is now sufficiently clear to justify nations taking prompt action. It is vital that all nations identify cost-effective steps that they can take now, to contribute to substantial and long-term reduction in net global greenhouse gas emissions.'[16]

Many scientists in the US have made it abundantly clear that there is now sufficient evidence of global warming to warrant action. In 2003, both the American Geophysical Union and American Meteorological Society declared that an artificially warming world was real and that it posed real dangers.

In 2004, a secret report commissioned by the Pentagon defense advisor, Andrew Marshall was obtained by *The Observer* newspaper and it predicted that climate change could have dire consequences in many parts of the world. The report predicted that there could be massive droughts affecting the US Midwest. Other changes could lead to wars over water in many parts of the world resulting in massive numbers of people migrating to richer countries in order to survive. Interestingly, but not surprisingly, the document was suppressed by the White House.[17]

The following year, 2005, the American Association for the

---

15. Jim Hansen, 'The Threat to the Planet', *The New York Review*, 13 July 2006, page 14.
16. David Adams, 'US scientists pile on pressure over climate change', *The Guardian*, 8 June 2005, page 4.
17. Mark Townsend and Paul Harris, 'Now the Pentagon tells Bush: climate change will destroy us', *The Observer*, 22 February 2004, page 3.

Advancement of Science joined with other Academies of Science from Britain, Japan, Germany and China in a statement saying that 'there is now strong evidence that global warming is occurring.'[18] In May 2006, the Climate Change Science Program, the co-ordinating group on climate change for the Bush administration declared that it had found 'clear evidence of human influences on climate systems'.[19]

Seattle's mayor Greg Nickels, together with 131 mayors from other cities including New York city, have agreed to implement Kyoto in their own cities. On 1 June 2005, a study by the *New York Times* and CBS News poll found that while people in the United States are overwhelmingly opposed to higher federal taxes on gasoline, 55% of those polled would accept higher taxes if the additional revenue was used to address global warming and to make the US less dependent on foreign oil for its energy supply.[20]

Without naming President George Bush, the Republican mayor of New York, Michael Bloomberg, in a speech to medical graduates at John Hopkins University School of Medicine in May 2006, criticised the way science has been manipulated to discredit the threat of global warming. He stated that 'despite the near-unanimity in the scientific community, there's now a movement, driven by ideology and short-term economics, to ignore the evidence and discredit the reality of climate change'.[21]

On the scientific side, the US National Academy of Sciences has made it clear that greenhouse gases are accumulating in the earth's atmosphere as a result of human activity and that it is causing surface air temperatures and ocean temperatures to rise. They have called for immediate steps for reducing greenhouse

18. Gregg Easterbrook, 'Finally Feeling the Heat', *The New York Times*, 24 May 2006, www.nytimes.com2006/05/24 page 1 of 3.
19. Ibid, page 2 of 3.
20. Louis Uchitelle and Megan Thee, 'Americans Are Cautiously Open to Gas Tax Rise, Poll Shows', *The New York Times*, 28 February, 2006. www.nytimes.com/2006/02/28/national/28, page 1 and 2.
21. Diane Cardwell, 'In Speech to Medical Graduates, Bloomberg Diverges From G.O.P. Line', *The New York Times*, 26 May 2006. www.nytimes.com/2006/05/26/ Page 2 of 2.

gas emissions immediately. The American Meteorological Society, the American Geophysical Union and the American Association for the Advancement of Science have issued similar statements.[22] What is more important is that ordinary people are beginning to feel that the climate is changing. This is true for people living in the great US plains. The prairies are no longer covered for months under a coat of snow.

A study by the federal Climate Change Science Programme in the US in May 2006 concluded that the earth's atmosphere was getting warmer. This finding is significant because skeptics have seized on the fact that satellite data has not recorded any noteworthy rise in temperature. This report stated that 'there is no longer a discrepancy in the rate of global average temperature increase for the surface compared with higher levels in the atmosphere'.[23] The report went on to conclude that global warming was taking place and this could not be explained by natural processes alone but had to be brought on by humans burning coal and oil.

On 30 August 2006, an agreement was reached between the Democratic-controlled Legislature of California and the Republican Governor, Arnold Schwartznegger, which calls for a 25% reduction of carbon dioxide emissions by 2020. This will involve reducing emissions from ulitities, oil refineries and cement plants. The ground work for enforcing the legislation begins immediately. The lead agency for determining emissions and penalties for non-compliance will be the California Air Resources Board. The controls will begin in 2012 with the aim of reducing emissions to 1990 levels by 2020. Incentives are included in the bill to help business reach these targets. The sponsor of the bill, Fabian Nunez, believes that this is merely the first step. Her goal is that California will be carbon free. While some business people predict that industries will move elsewhere where there are no restrictions, be that North Carolina or China, four out of

22. Poly Ghazi, 'A storm brewing', *The Guardian*, 6 July 2005, page 13 (supplement).
23. Alec Russell 'US report admits pollution to blame for climate', *The Irish Independent*, 4 May 2006, page 13.

five respondents to a recent poll in California, conducted by the Public Policy Institute of California, believe that urgent action is needed on climate change. Many realise that California is vulnerable to climate change. The state depends on the snow packs on the Sierra Nevada for much of its water supply. A study by the National Academy of Science, conducted in 2004, predicts that if global warming continues the snow on the mountains may be reduced by at least 29% by the end of this century.[24]

One initiative which will be closely watched is the Californian Hydrogen Highway Network. This is planned to be in operation by 2010 and will facilitate those who are opting for hydrogen operated cars which do not give off greenhouse gases. All these cars emit is water vapour and some traces of the lubricant used in the engine. California hopes to have between 150 and 200 hydrogen fueling stations which will roughly mean one fueling station every 20 miles along California's 21 interstate freeways.

The problem with using hydrogen as an energy source is that, while it is very abundant in the universe and here on planet earth, it always comes chemically bonded with some other element or molecule. The water molecule contains two atoms of hydrogen and one atom of oxygen. When one electrolyses the water the hydrogen gas is released. At the moment this is an expensive process and most often it is fossil fuel that is used to make the hydrogen available. But there are many experiments under way aimed at isolating hydrogen without using either fossil fuel or a nuclear source.

It is important to remember that at present it is difficult to store hydrogen. Though it provides more power per unit of weight than petrol, it provides much less power per unit of volume and this creates problems with regard to sufficient storage space. There are also legitimate safety concerns. Hydrogen does

---

24. Felicity Barringer, 'Officials Reach California Deal to Cut Emissions', *The New York Times*, *www.nytimes.com/2006/31/washington/31warming.html?* pages 1 and 2.

not have a smell, so it is difficult to detect leaks. It would be essential to design leak-proof tanks to store the high-pressure hydrogen. There is on-going research into developing sensors to detect hydrogen leaks. Obviously this and other alternative fuel options would benefit from public money to kick-start vital research. The sensors must also be developed to shut down the entire system if an accident occurred. The fear that hydrogen will explode and catch fire, like what seemed to have happened to the airship *Hindenburg* in New York in 1937, is still strong in the public imagination. The scenario is not accurate. In the case of the *Hindenburg* the fire began with the highly inflammable cellulose and aluminum skin of the balloon. This is what did all the damage. In fact the hydrogen was quickly dispersed into the air.[25]

In August 2005, seven northeastern states in the US agreed to set up a trading system to deal with carbon dioxide. While the agreement is weak when one compares it with the obligations which the EU have undertaken, it is a landmark agreement and may force the hand of the federal government to take decisive action in relation to curbing global emissions of greenhouse gases.[26]

The US Supreme Court may yet intervene in the debate about global warming. In May 2006, in a case Massachusetts *v* EPA, prominent scientists urged the Supreme Court to hear the following case. It revolved around whether the US Clean Air Act compels the EPA to restrict greenhouse gas emissions. The Clean Air Act states that the head of the EPA 'shall' regulate emissions of new vehicles 'which in his judgement cause or contribute to air pollution which may reasonably be anticipated to endanger public health or welfare'. Until then the EPA had decided not to regulate greenhouse gas emissions from the transport sector under the statute. The reason they gave for their stance was that there was still uncertainty about climate change.

25. Timothy Gardner, 'UPDATE – US Northeast States to Act on CO2', 16 August 2006, Reuters, know now.
26. Ibid.

They stated that if Congress had intended to include this in the bill they would have said so explicitly when it was amended in 1990.

The EPA argued that carbon dioxide emissions lie outside its remit. Massachusetts and 11 other states, including California and New York, disagreed and fought the battle through the courts. The States lost by 2 to 1 in the US Court of Appeals in 2001. The plaintiffs decided to appeal to the Supreme Court because according to the main lawyer for Massachusetts, James Milkey, the EPA never applied the right standards – endangerment. Scientists claim that the Court of Appeals cherry picked all the uncertainties in the National Academy of Sciences report on climate change. They refused to act on the consensus that exists now in the scientific community about the facts of global warming and the inevitable negative consequences.

Even if the Supreme Court decided to hear this case and sided with Massachusetts, it may not compel the EPA to begin regulating greenhouse gas emissions. Nevertheless it would be a great victory and would send out the message that climate change is serious and needs to be addressed urgently.[27]

*Industry beginning to take global warming seriously*
Industry in the US is also beginning to see non-fossil fuel energy sources as a business opportunity. In May 2005, General Electric, the fifth largest company in the US, announced that it would double its research and development budget for clean energy technologies by 2010.[28] Timberland, the outdoor clothing company, has also studied ways to reduce its carbon emissions. It looked at various options. These included building a wind farm in the Dominican Republic, buying power generated from renewable sources and, finally, expanding its use of solar energy. The company decided that they would take each of the options. The research showed that the bulk of greenhouse gases associated

27. Jessica Marshall, 'Let the Supreme Court decide', *NewScientist*, 27 May 2006, page 8.
28. Poly Ghari, op. cit., page 13.

with the manufacture of their leather boots came from cows producing methane. The company chairman Jeffrey B. Swartz said that while he shared concerns over global warming the main reason why the company had opted for greener policies was economic. Saving energy makes good economic sense and gives them an advantage over their competitors.[29]

Despite the inaction of the Bush administration on global warming, businesses in the US could do much more to cut carbon emissions and cut costs in the process. The US is responsible for 25% of all carbon dioxide emissions into the atmosphere each year. Instead of dropping, emission rates are rising to such an extent that the US Department of Energy predicts that carbon dioxide emissions could rise to 8 billion tonnes by 2030.

To date only 86 companies in the US have signed up to the voluntary EPA programme to cut carbon emissions. Alan Nogee, director of the clean energy programme at the Union of Concerned Scientists, has stated that 'there is a lot of inertia in the economy, and many companies have their heads in the sand, wishing and hoping that somehow the overwhelming consensus among scientists is going to go away'.[30]

*Churches and Global Warming*

Early in 2005 over 1,000 evangelical ministers signed a letter to President Bush calling on the White House to be more proactive on environmental issues, including global warming. They told the President that caring for creation and promoting a sustainable environment was part of the duty of every Christian.

Eighty-six leaders of Evangelical churches pledged to back a major global warming initiative in February 2006 because they believe that 'millions of people could die in this century because of climate change, most of them our poorest global neighbours'.[31]

29. Jad Mouawad, 'The Greener Guys', *The New York Times*, May 30, 2006. www.nytimes.com/2006/05/30/business/30carbon.html page 1 of 4.
30. ibid, page 2 of 4.
31. Laurie Goodstein, '86 Evangelical Leaders Join to Fight Global Warming.' *The New York Times*, 8 February 2006. www.nytimes.com/2006/02/08/national/08war .html page 1 of 3.

The signatories include the presidents of 39 evangelical colleges, leaders of the Salvation Army, other aid groups and also some pastors from what are called mega-churches. Rich Warren, who wrote the best seller *The Purpose-Driven Life*, also added his name to the document. The statement calls for reductions in carbon dioxide emissions through 'cost effective, market-based mechanisms'. This approach reflects the fact that many evangelicals are pro-business and see market forces as the solution to almost every problem. The statement commended companies whom they felt were taking some positive action with regard to climate change. These include Shell, General Electric, Conergy, Duke Energy and DuPont which have taken some innovative measures to address climate change.

*Technical fixes*
One of the technical fixes which is proposed to reduce the level of carbon dioxide in the air is called carbon capture and storage (CCS) technology. Proponents of this technology feel that it could be used to sequester carbon from the atmosphere and thereby slow down climate change while allowing us to continue to use fossil fuels in a profligate way. It is like having your cake and eating it.

The most recent comment on CCS from the International Panel on Climate Change is somewhat skeptical about the effectiveness of this technology. They concede that by the year 2050, CCS could sequester only 20-40 percent of global carbon dioxide emissions from large generating points like power plants. To do this you would need to have places to store the sequestered carbon. Some people have suggested that old mines might be suitable but these are not always situated close to where the carbon is generated. The oceans have also been suggested as a possible storage option. Injecting the carbon dioxide into the sea to a depth of 3,000 metres, where it would be expected to form carbon pools, would be very expensive and would have huge consequences for the acidity of the oceans if anything went wrong. Even now there is increase acidification of the oceans due to the huge volume of carbon dioxide which is being produced. As the carbon dioxide dissolves in the oceans it increases the acidification which in turn puts pressure on marine creatures, especially shell fish. It may also kill much of the microscopic plankton on which the marine food chain depends. The knock-on effect of the acidification on almost every marine creature and even humankind could be immense. Scientists have calculated if you liquidised our carbon dioxide output we would need to inject 50 cubic kilometers into the earth's crust each year if we go down the sequestering route.[32]

CCS of course would not be effective in reducing the emissions from vehicles unless vehicles began using alternative energy like hydrogen or electricity generated from renewable energy sources.

*Natural Fixes*
Enormous amounts of carbon are naturally stored in trees and other plants. This takes place through the process of photosynthesis whereby plants absorb carbon dioxide from the atmosphere and store it as sugar, starch and cellulose while releasing oxygen back into the atmosphere. Young trees are the optimum carbon sink as they absorb more carbon than mature trees during their growing phase. When trees are felled and burned they release carbon back into the atmosphere. If, however, dead trees are allowed to rot slowly, they both enrich the soil and act as a carbon sink. The important thing to remember is that we need to plant more native trees in Ireland, and right across the globe, especially in the tropics where rainforests have been destroyed in recent decades.

---

32. Tim Flannery, op. cit., page 254.

# CHAPTER 5

# The Kyoto Protocol

*Kyoto Meeting 1997*

Climate change figured prominently on the agenda of the United Nations Conference on Environment and Development, popularly known as the Earth Summit, which took place in Rio De Janiero in June 1992. A certain amount of ground work had already taken place at two important international meetings. The first scientific conference to get to grips with climate change took place in Villach in Austria in 1985. This was followed three years later with a conference in Toronto attended by scientists and policy makers. This latter conference issued a call for action to reduce the release of greenhouse gases into the atmosphere.

Climate change figured frequently in the speeches of the heads of state at the Rio Meeting. As a result, 154 nations signed the UN Framework Convention on Climate Change. The purpose of the Convention was to reduce the level of 18 greenhouse gases in the atmosphere and thus limit the damage that global warming was doing and might do to the earth. The target year was 2000 when countries were expected to lower their greenhouse gas output to below 1990 levels. It was an unrealistic goal. The effectiveness of the Convention was undermined when the US administration under President George Bush Sr pandered to the powerful fossil fuel lobby in the US and refused to set specific targets for reducing greenhouse gas emissions globally. At that time it was estimated that while the US represented only 6% of the world's population it was responsible for 25% of greenhouse gas emissions.

A slight change in the US approach to global warming happened with the election of President Bill Clinton in 1992. As a result of this shift the parties to the UN Convention on Climate Change that met in Geneva in July 1996 produced a strong statement committing industrialised countries to negotiate a legally binding international protocol to reduce their greenhouse gas emissions. While the targets set in the declaration were very modest, at least things were moving in the right direction.

The attempt by the international community to deal with global warming received another boost at the UN Conference on Climate Change which took place in Kyoto in December 1997. The scientists who where members of the International Panel on Climate Change (IPCC) called for at least a 60% cut in greenhouse gas emission to stabilise global temperatures. Those attending the meeting could only agree on a 5.2%-7% reduction on 1990 levels by 2012. While countries in the European Union were willing to give more, the US administration dragged its feet because of domestic pressure from powerful corporations.

In the run up to the Kyoto Conference a group of industries known as the Carbon Club ran advertisements to block any US involvement in Kyoto. Companies, especially those involved in the energy sector were afraid that their profits would fall if there were a drop in fossil fuel consumption. The dominant group in the Carbon Club was the Global Climate Coalition. This was a 'Who's Who' of US business and industry. It included such names as Exxon Mobil, Shell, Ford, General Motors and leading coal, steel, aluminum and energy corporations. They used all kinds of tactics – corporate PR, psychology, mass media manipulation techniques and political muscle to force politicians and opinion makers to do their will. The campaign set up a series of font groups, which funded so-called 'independent scientists', nurtured politically conservative and far-right think-tanks, and sought to discredit individuals and groups that were calling for action on climate change. One individual who has poured cold water on global warming is the Australian scientist Patrick Michaels. They quoted his work and then urged that governments in effect do nothing because curbing global warming may have adverse effects on business. Patrick Michael's research has, in part, been funded by the Cyprus Mineral Company, Edison Electric Institute and the German Coal Mining Association (*The Guardian*, October 29, 1997). In Australia, A$400,000 was donated by transnational corporations such as Rio Tinto, Exxon Mobil and Australian Aluminium Council to groups who were opposed to Australia signing up to to Kyoto.[1] Interestingly a number of companies, like DuPont, British Petroleum and eventually Texaco, pulled out of the Global Climate Coalition. It collapsed in March 2000.

While the Clinton administration signed the Kyoto Protocol, the Byrd-Hagel resolution passed in 1997 urged the Senate to reject any treaty that might damage the US economy. The resolution was passed by the US Senate by 95 to 0.

The Kyoto Protocol came into effect on 16 February 2005, ninety days after the Russian Duma (Parliament) voted in favour of ratification. In December 2005, the 130 signatories to the protocol and other nations gathered in Buenos Aires to celebrate the event and to look to the future beyond 2012. It was a sobering event for a number of reasons. Many of the countries that had signed up to the Kyoto Protocol realised that they could not comply with what they agreed even though the carbon cuts were very small in comparison to what needs to be done to stabilise climates. Furthermore, Kyoto did not deal with economies like India and China which are showing double digit economic growth and are becoming major polluters. Finally, the United States, the richest nation and largest economy in the world, is still sitting on the sidelines.

It is important in the future to get commitments to reduce fossil fuel emissions from countries like India, China and Brazil which have increased their greenhouse gas emissions in the past decade.[2] But countries in the Minority World will have to cut the greenhouse gas emissions by 60% to 80% in order to ensure that

---

1. Tim Flannery, op. cit., page 227.
2. Larry Rother and Andrew C Revkin, 'Cheers, and Concern, for New Climate Pact', *The New York Times*, 13 December 2005. www.nytimes. com 13/12/04.

the carbon dioxide levels in the atmosphere do not exceed 500 ppm.

One of the main breakthroughs of the Kyoto Protocol is that it was the first time that industrialised countries agreed to implement mandatory cuts on carbon dioxide emissions. It also allows countries to buy carbon credits to meet their treaty obligations by investing in emission control in other non-industrialised countries. Those who negotiated the Kyoto Protocol realised that it is merely the first step if the worst excesses of climate change are not to be realised. Carbon trading works like this. A regulator sets emission limits for each country for the various greenhouse gases. Then these permits are given on a proportional basis to industries which are already in place. These permits may also be auctioned. Industries which cannot meet their targets can buy permits to pollute from countries or companies who are below their target.

Those who opposed Kyoto often claim that the findings of the International Panel on Climate Change (IPCC) are skewed and incorrect. This is difficult to believe since the membership of the IPCC is comprised of scientists and government officials. The various groups in the energy industry are well represented by representatives from the US and the oil producing nations. For this reason, the reports from the IPCC often represent only the lowest common denominator position. Nevertheless, their pronouncements are becoming more and more challenging.

In December 2005, the United Nations held another Framework Convention on Climate Change in Montreal, Canada. This was meant as a follow-on from the Kyoto Protocol. Once again the US, through its chief negotiator Dr Harian L. Watson objected to any form of international agreement which was not voluntary or market-based. He told *The New York Times*, 'we would certainly not agree to the US being part of legally binding targets and timetable agreements post 2012.' *The New*

*York Times*, branded his approach as 'shameless foot dragging' for which the Bush administration 'deserves only censure'.[3]

In June 2005, the European Union endorsed a plan to further reduce greenhouse gas emission by between 15% and 30% by the year 2020. Many commentators are skeptical about the feasibility of this aspiration given that 11 of the 15 members before enlargement had actually increased their emissions. Some countries like Spain have increased by over 40%. Ireland, of course, was not far behind at 23%.[4]

One interesting outcome of the Montreal meeting was to focus attention on how quickly the carbon trading concept can turn into a farce. The point of any greenhouse gas initiative is to reduce emissions but many are concerned that the exercise has been turned into a carbon accountancy scam driven by large companies who are poised to make money out of the carbon trading system rather than using it to reduce carbon emissions.

At the Montreal Conference on climate change in December 2005, Geg Nickels, the mayor of Seattle, said that 'the issue of climate disruption has become very clear to Americans. The damage done to New Orleans has affected people very deeply and they want action.' He stated that Seattle would meet the 7% reduction in greenhouse gas emissions which would have applied to the US if it had signed up to Kyoto. He claimed that 192 mayors representing over 40 million people in the US were also intent on pursuing the Kyoto limits. Nine of the states in the northeastern part of the US are working on an initiative to cut greenhouse gas emission.[5]

---

3. Jim Motavalli, 'The Montreal Talks: A lot of Hot Air', www.emagazine.com/view/?2989&priintview&image12/14/2005 page 1 of 2.

4. Ibid.

5 David Adam, 'Beckett urges targets to fight climate change', *The Guardian*, 7 December 2005. www.guardian.co.uk/print12/07/2005. page 1 and 2.

*Ireland and Kyoto*

At Kyoto, Ireland was one of the few wealthy nations that received permission to increase its 'greenhouse' gas emissions. We claimed that, since we had not been industrialised in the 19th century, we should be allowed more leeway than other industrial countries. We were allowed to increase our greenhouse gas emissions by 13% above the 1990 levels by the year 2012.

The gallop of the Celtic Tiger from the mid-1990s meant that by 1998 Ireland had already exceeded these greenhouse gas emission levels. It was clear that emissions would continue to escalate unless there was a serious change in energy policy. In 1997, a study by the Economic and Social Research Institute (ESRI) predicted that, unless energy policies changed dramatically, Ireland's greenhouse gas emissions would rise to 28% by the year 2010. But no change came. In fact the opposite happened. Instead of promoting alternative energies like wind or wave, the government built a peat-fired plant in Edenderry, Co Offaly. This 120 megawatt planet emits over 600,000 tonnes of carbon dioxide into the atmosphere each year.

In August 2000, the Environmental Protection Agency published a report entitled *Emissions of Atmospheric Pollutants in Ireland 1990-1998*. It stated that Ireland had already exceeded its emission targets for 2010 by the year 1998 since greenhouse gas emissions had grown by 18% in eight years. The annual rate of greenhouse gas emission was then over 4%. In response, the Department of the Environment published the *National Climate Change Strategy* to curb greenhouse gas emissions in November 2000. Very little happened. Among the initiatives mentioned were an unspecified tax on fossil fuel, the closure or conversion of the Moneypoint coal-fired power station and reductions in the number of animals in the national herd. Later the Minister dropped this commitment, claiming the move to gas would mean that 80% of our generating power was dependent on natural gas and that would make Ireland extremely vulnerable if we were importing gas from Siberia. An Taisce has describe

Moneypoint as 'the single most problematic greenhouse gas and acid-rain emitter in Ireland'.[6]

The *National Climate Change Strategy*, lamely admitted that 'transport is generally proving to be the most difficult sector in which to achieve controls on greenhouse gas emissions in most countries due to the rising vehicle numbers and increasing travel.' Chapter five of the Report dealt with transport. It is vague and aspirational. The development of rail transport was mentioned on few occasions but, for the authors of this Report, transport meant – road transport.

After the Report was published, I attempted to find out whether any Government Department or Agency had calculated what the extra emissions of greenhouse gases would be coming from the road building programme. Presumably the need for these motorways springs from research on the increased volume of vehicles on the roads, therefore it ought to be quite easy to quantify what the increase in greenhouse gases would be. I called the National Roads Authority and spoke to a very helpful person who informed me that the NRA had not quantified what the increase greenhouse gas load will be. Their Environmental Impact Studies (EIS) looked at local levels of air pollution which will follow in the wake of the motorway building programme, but they had no figures on the increase in greenhouse gas emissions.

In July 2002, the Irish government produced another document in preparation for the World Summit on Sustainable Development scheduled for Johannesburg from August 26-September 4, 2002. The Report entitled *Making Ireland Sustainable* acknowledged that, according to the Environmental Protection Agency, Ireland's emissions of greenhouse gases in the year 2000 were already 23.7% above 1990 levels. Under a 'business-as-usual' scenario they would increase to 27% by 2010. Once again this document was heavy on spin and what must be done. Rather feebly, it informed the readers that 'it has always been

6. Frank McDonald, 'Power Struggle', *The Irish Times*, Weekend Review, 14 January 2006, page 2.

recognised that, with no action, Ireland would rapidly and substantially exceed its (Kyoto) Protocol targets'. It went on to state
that 'significant action' is required over this decade to limit the
rise in emissions to 13%.[7] The document did promise to pursue
'appropriate tax measures, prioritising carbon dioxide emission'. These were to be 'introduced on a phased basis across all
sectors, taking into account social and economic activities'.[8]

This particular commitment was abandoned in 2004. The ex-
cuse given was that it would be too onerous on the poor even
though the ESRI disagreed and had suggested ways of implementing this tax that would not hurt poor people.

One of the most disappointing statistics in a recent publication on energy trends is that cars with a 1.2 litre engine or less
have shown a steady decline in ownership since 1990. Cars with
engine sizes larger than 1.2 litre have shown a steady increase so
that the bulk of cars on the Irish roads in 2004 were in the 1.2 to
1.5 litre engine size. This means greater greenhouse gas emissions.[9]

A report published by the European Environment Agency
(EEA) in March 2006, entitled *Transport and Environment: Facing
a Dilemma 2006*, confirms that greenhouse gas emissions from
the transport sector have increased at greater speed in Ireland
than in any other European country. Between 1990 and 2003 pollution from cars increased by 130%. The average increase for the
same period in most other European countries was around 23%.
The director of the agency Professor Jacqueline McGlade stated
that major policy initiatives were essential, if Ireland was to
achieve a drop in emissions. These included using taxation, toll
charges and more investment in biofuel.[10]

7. 'Meeting Kyoto commitment seen as a "core" challenge', *The Irish
Times*, July 26, 2002, page 5.
8. Liam Reid, 'Taxpayers will pay high price for broken promises on
Kyoto', *The Irish Times*, April 3, 2006, page 15.
9.*Energy in Ireland 1990 – 2004, Trends, issues, forecasts and indicators*,SEI
Sustainable Energy Ireland, Energy Policy Statistical Support Unit,
page 53.
10. Jamie Smyth, 'Ireland's greenhouse gases show fastest rise', *The Irish
Times*, March 28, 2006, page 1.

Towards the end of 2002 the Irish government began to wake up to the fact that their unwillingness to take any effective steps to curb greenhouse gas emission, either by way of taxes on fossil fuels or subsidies to promote alternative energy sources, might cost them dearly. Under the Kyoto Protocol, Ireland was allowed to increase its greenhouse gas emissions by 13% above the 1990 levels. Research by the Environmental Protection Agency and consultants DIW Berlin discovered that by 2001 Ireland has achieved a 31% increase in greenhouse gas emissions. It was back to 23% in 2004 not because of government policy but because of the closure of Irish Fertilisers in Arklow and Irish Steel in Cork.

Iva Pocock, writing in *The Irish Times*, points out that the former finance minister effectively 'binned' the National Climate Change Strategy when he reneged on a promise to introduce a carbon tax. She pointed out that economist John Fitzgerald denounced the action, stating that it leaves no effective instrument for meeting the Kyoto targets. Regrettably, there were no environmentalists protesting loudly about this irresponsible action which was taken, probably after pressure from some vested interest group.[11] With such ineffective political leadership it is not surprising that greenhouse gas emissions began climbing again in 2006. The breakdown of emissions in 2006 were as follows: transport accounts for 17%, agriculture 30%, industry 10%, home heating 10% and energy production 25%.[12] *Per capita* emissions in Ireland are the highest in the EU.

An EPA Report in 2006 showed that Ireland's emissions grew by 0.45 % in 2004. This means that they had increased by 23.5% on 1990 figures. The largest contribution to emissions is from agriculture at 29 per cent. This is mainly methane from cattle and other ruminants. Energy production accounts for 25% and transport is up to 17.5%.[13] In May 2006, the Central Statistics

11. Iva Pocock, 'We need to clear the air', *The Irish Times*, 13 November 2004, page 9.
12. Donal Buckley, 'Putting Ireland out of business is no answer to climate change', *The Irish Times*, 13 February 2006, page 14.
13. Frank McDonald, 'Ireland's greenhouse gas emissions up', *The Irish Times*, 17February 2006, page 10.

Office figures indicated that between 1997 and 2004 there was a 7% increase in greenhouse gas emission. Once again the most significant increase was in the transport section which grew by a staggering 62% during the same period. The reason for the sharp increase in greenhouse gas emissions is that the number of cars on Irish roads increased from 939,022 to 1,582,833 between 1994 and 2004. The number of goods vehicles, including trucks and vans, went from 135,809 to 268,082 in the same period. The transport sector is now responsible for 40% of the energy used in Ireland and, instead of decreasing, it is increasing by 8% each year.[14]

One of the main causes of increase in greenhouse gas production in 2004/5 was the increased cement production to service the growing building trade.

If we continue with our present do-nothing policies Ireland could be back up in the high twenties by 2012. Since fines are part of the Kyoto Protocol, Ireland could be facing penalties as high as €1 billion. Alternatively we could buy permits to pollute from other countries. This would cost almost €200 million per year.[15] An industry like Aughinish Alumina in the Shannon Estuary will have to pay €45 million each year between 2008 and 2012 to meet its greenhouse gas targets.[16] As I have written above, the total cost to industry and the economy for the five year period of the Protocol could be as high as €1 billion.

The Department of the Environment finally woke up to the cost factor in not meeting our Kyoto targets but it seems that the mindset of the Department of Finance and Enterprise, Trade and Employment is to put industry ahead of everything else.[17] Mr Buckley, the head of environment policy at IBEC, wrote an article for *The Irish Times* which effectively told the government not

---

14. ibid
15. Liam Reid, 'Kyoto shortfall to cost Government 185 milllion euro', *The Irish Times*, 31 December 20004, page 4.
16. Treacy Hogan, 'Taxpayers faced with a 300 million euro bill over gas emissions', *Irish Independent*, 29 March 2006, page 11.
17. Liam Reid, 'Kyoto may cost state 5 billion euro', *The Sunday Tribune*, 2 February 2002, page 11

to burden industry with any requirements in the fight against global warming.[18] Strong lobbying from business interests has effectively prevented any carbon tax in the EU even though the idea was suggested as far back as 1991.[19]

*Carbon Permits*

In response to the Kyoto agreement the European Union set up an emission trading systems (ETS) which puts a limit on the amount of greenhouse gases a country is allowed to emit. The idea behind the scheme is to limit emissions of carbon dioxide so that European countries can meet their Kyoto targets. These permits were distributed to 11,500 businesses in the EU, mainly in the energy generation business and those industries involved in making cement. These industries are responsible for one half of the carbon dioxide emission from Europe. Under the ETS each country is expected to devise a National Allocation Plan which will be sent to Brussels. Included in this plan will be the number of tonnes of carbon dioxide which the polluter will be allowed to emit. In Ireland, the lion's share of the permit went to the Electricity Supply Board (ESB). They got a permit to emit 11 million tonnes with an allocation of 4.4 million tonnes for Moneypoint power station alone.

Many commentators are critical of the Irish government for giving very generous allotments to companies which in practice allows them to continue polluting or, alternatively, to sell their permits to other businesses. It is also a major subsidy to polluters which will give them significant financial advantages over companies which do not receive any permit. The value of a permit to emit one tonne of carbon dioxide in April 2006 was €22. The price of permits is expected to increase in the years to come as countries' permits to pollute are reduced each year and the cost of fossil fueld increases.

The organisation *Feasta*, which promotes sustainable living

18. ibid.
19. Pat Finnegan, 'IBEC full of 'hot air' in its take on facing up to Kyoto', *The Irish Times*, 16 February 2006, page 16.

in Ireland, has argued that the Emission Trading System (ETS) should be much more democratic if it is to work in a fair and equable way. In a submission to the Department of the Environment in November 2005, *Feasta* pointed to a report by the Energy Research Centre of the Netherlands (ECN) entitled *Carbon Dioxide Price Dynamics: The Implications of EU Emissions Trading for the Price of Electricity*. The study found that despite the fact that large corporations received a free allocation allowance, the companies passed on the market value of their carbon emission allocation to their customers. As a consequence of their action, the price of electricity increased by almost one third.

The report concluded that the free allocation of emission allowances was a very questionable policy option for a number of reasons. John Fitzgerald from ESRI estimates that the give-away could be worth as much as €1,350 million if the price to emit a tonne of carbon dioxide was €20. Rather than acting as a carrot to encourage industry to reduce carbon dioxide emissions the scheme will encourage the owners of polluting plants to keep them in operation in order to be eligible for this subsidy which benefits polluting industries by between €200 million and €1 billion over a five year period.[20]

Some economists believe that the state should auction the carbon dioxide pollution permits. This would raise revenue for the state without unduly pushing up the price of energy. Part of this revenue could then be used by government agencies to increase social welfare payments so that those most vulnerable from the increased price of energy would be facilitated. The Director of Friends of the Earth Ireland, Oisín Coghlan has also criticised the government's handling of carbon credits. According to him 'this is the ultimate stealth tax. The government has replaced the polluter-pays principle with the public-pays principle.'[21]

An alternative approach, in fact the one supported by *Feasta*,

20. Liam Reid, 'Limits on greenhouse gases to be set in effort to cut levels', *The Irish Times*, 20 March 2006, page 1.
21. Frank McDonald, 'Free carbon credits scheme condemned', *The Irish Times*, 17 July 2006, page 4.

is to give all the national allowance to pollute to all the citizens of the country on an equal *per capita* basis of Transferable Energy Quotas, or TEQs. The advantage of this scheme is that all the carbon dioxide emissions would be accounted for, not just from dirty industries. The recipient could sell the TEQ allocation to a bank, post office or credit union. The price received would depend on how well the European economy was performing and on its demand for fossil fuel. Businesses which are dealing in important fossil fuel – gas, coal or oil – or buying these fuels from producers within the EU, would have to buy enough TEQs from the banks to cover the emissions their products would release into the environment when used. They would hand the TEQs they had purchased to Customs, if the fuel was imported, or to EU producers for EU produced fuel. A corps of inspectors would be required to police the process to ensure, for example, that the amount of fuel delivered by the EU producer was in accordance with the TEQs received.

Another advantage of opting for personal permits is, as the right to emit carbon is diminished over the years to stabilise the climate, the price of permits would rise and individuals and households would benefit, not the big corporations. The higher income from the permits would help people meet fuel bills which will be increase dramatically in the future.[22]

*Britain*
Britain had pledged to reduce the UK carbon dioxide emissions by 20% by 2010. It appeared in March 2006 that the UK would not meet this target. The most it could achieve, according to the Environment Secretary, was a 15% to 18% reduction. The failure to meet the target is a major embarrassment to the Prime Minister who had pledged to make global warming a priority both when he was in the chair of the G8 group and when Britain had the presidency of the EU. It seems to be the case that his passionate commitment to reducing carbon emission has not been

22. Richard Dowthwaite, 'Climate Change', *The Local Planet*, February-April, 2006, page 36.

translated into viable programmes. The Environment Secretary blamed the lapse on economic growth and increased demand for electricity. This forced the suppliers to move from using less polluting gas-fired power stations to the much dirtier coal burning power stations.

The review made some suggestions to reduce carbon emissions by between 7 million and 12 million tones. This includes increasing energy efficiency and using biomass. The government is also encouraging small businesses and even schools to use solar panels and small wind turbines to create, what they call, 'micropower' systems.[23]

Unfortunately, Prime Minister Blair softened his stand on climate change during a speech in Davos in Switzerland in 2005. In an address to the World Economic Forum, Mr Blair said that climate change was not universally accepted. He went on to say that the evidence was still disputed. The dangers from climate change have been 'clearly and persuasively advocated' by a large number of 'entirely independent voices. They are the majority. The majority is not always right but they deserve to be listened to.'[24]

*Contraction and Convergence*

Beyond the Kyoto process there is a growing support for another approach which is known as Contraction and Convergence (C&C). At the heart of this proposal, which has been promoted for a decade by the British politician, Aubrey Meyer, is the idea that every individual has an equal right to emit greenhouse gases. It is often referred to as the 'right to pollute'. Each individual, no matter where he/she lived, could trade their emissions. At the moment people in rich countries emit 50 times or even 100 times more greenhouse gases than their counterparts in poorer countries. If this regime were put in place people in rich

23. Brian Adam and Terry Macalister, 'Government accused of pitiful failure to meet target for greenhouse gas emissions', *The Guardian*, 29 March 2006, page 14.
24. David Adam, 'Oil firms fund campaign to deny climate change', *The Guardian*, 27 January 2005, page 1.

countries would have to buy 'carbon' credits from people in poor countries. If this carbon economy got under way it would achieve a number of goals. Firstly, it would put pressure on rich countries to reduce their carbon footprints. Secondly, it would involve massive transfers of wealth from the rich countries to the poor countries.

The C&C approach would involve a number of steps. Firstly, the ground rules would need to be laid out at an international conference where there would be an agreement to place a 'cap' on carbon dioxide concentrations in the atmosphere worldwide. The next step would be to work out how quickly carbon dioxide emissions need to be cut back to reach the goal which has been set. Building on step 1 and 2, it would be necessary to estimate the total 'carbon budget' and then divide that among the world's population on a *per capita* basis.[25]

Like Kyoto, C&C envisages a carbon currency. However, the cut-backs envisaged are greater than those imposed under Kyoto which ranged only from 5% to 7% cut-backs. Given the crisis we are facing deep cuts may be the only way to bring about significant cuts in greenhouse gases by 2050. A major benefit from this approach is that it would narrow the gap between rich and poor countries. It would make capital available to promote a non-fossil fuel economy and it could be used to pay off Third World Debt. Because everyone on earth would be involved, the US administration could not claim that it favours 'free-rides' in poor countries which was one of their main reasons for rejecting Kyoto.[26]

25. Tim Flannery, op. cit., page 299-301.
26. Ibid page 300.

# CHAPTER 6

# *Is Nuclear Power the Solution to Global Warming?*

My own involvement in the debate about nuclear power goes back to the late 1970s and early 1980s when the Marcos government in the Philippines decided to built a nuclear power plant at Bataan, north of Manila on the Island of Luzon. A number of Filipino non-government organisations (NGOs) took a case to the Philippines Supreme Court to prevent the opening of the power plant. I was involved in that discussion through my membership of an NGO called *Lingod Tao Kalikasan*. The NGOs were delighted that the Supreme Court forbade National Power Corporation to begin generating electricity at the Bataan nuclear plant, just before the downfall of Mr Marcos in 1986. After the Marcos government was overthrown, a team of international inspectors visited the plant and declared it unsafe. The nuclear plant was built near a geological fault line. There were four active volcanoes within a range of thirty miles along with another volcano which was dormant. The latter was called Pinatubo and it erupted in 1992. It was considered one of the largest and most dangerous eruptions of the 20th century. The fate of the installation was sealed when the government of President Cory Aquino came into power in 1986. She banned nuclear power and enshrined the ban in the Philippines Constitution.

In 1999, I wrote a book called *Greening the Christian Millennium*. A chapter on nuclear power was called 'Downwind from Hiroshima and Chernobyl'. There I wrote that the dangers of nuclear power are not confined to nuclear weapons alone. It is important to realise that civilian nuclear power, in other words the use of nuclear power to generate electricity, is inextricably linked to a nuclear weapons programme. In the words of the

Swedish nobel prize winning physicist, Hannes Alven, the peaceful atom and military atom are 'Siamese twins'. As the Oxford Research Group write, 'civilian nuclear activities and nuclear weapons proliferation are intimately linked: one of the 'twins' cannot be promoted with the other spreading out of control.'[1] Currently about sixty countries in the world have civilian nuclear power plants. It is estimated that over the past forty years twenty of these countries have used their supposedly civilian nuclear facilities to undertake covert research on a weapons programme.[2] While the Bush Administration is condemning Iran's nuclear programme at the United Nations Security Council, they are actively engaged in researching new kinds of nuclear weapons which are in contravention of the Nuclear Non-Proliferation treaty. The Spratt-Fuse Prohibition in the US Congress forbade any funding for research and development of low-yield nuclear weapons. The reason for this was that these weapons would blur the distinction between conventional and nuclear weapons. The Bush administration has attempted to overturn this bill so that they can develop what are known as Robust Nuclear Earth Penetrators (RNEP). These could then be used to bomb bunkers where enemy headquarters were located or important weaponry was stored. If the US continues to develop these weapons, other nations like Russia and China will follow their example and add a new, potentially horrendous danger to humans and the rest of creation.[3]

1. Chris Abbott, Paul Rogers and John Sloboda, 'Global Responses to Global Threats: Sustainable Security for the 21st Century', *Oxford Research Group*, 2006, page 12, Oxford Research Group, 51 Plantation Road, Oxford OX2 6JE, United Kingdom.
2. Nuclear Weapon Archive, 'Nuclear Weapon Nations and Arsenals' www.nuclearweaponarchive.org/Nwfaq/Nfaq7.html; *Institute for Science and International Security*, 'Nuclear Weapons Program Worldwide: An Historical Overview', www.isis-online.org/mapproject/introduction.html>
3. David West, 'Proliferate This', *The Ecologist*, July-August, 2006, pages 16-18.

*Accidents*

The nuclear industry received a major set back with the serious accident at Three Mile Island in 1979 in Pennsylvania. The biggest blow to the nuclear industry came seven years later, on 26 April 1986, when an accident occurred at a nuclear power station in Chernobyl. The explosion hurled 190 tonnes of uranium and graphite into the atmosphere. This radioactive material, the equivalent of 400 Hiroshima bombs, was carried by the wind all over Western Europe and contaminated an area of 150,000 square miles.[4] The cloud reached Ireland two days later, bringing its radioactive load of iodine -131, caesium -137, caesium - 134, ruthenium -103, and ruthenium -106 to the country. When it rained on that weekend, the levels of caesium 137 increased forty-fold. Sheep from upland areas of Donegal and Mayo are still regularly tested for radiation, as these areas experienced more radiation from the Chernobyl explosion than anywhere else.[5]

Undoubtedly, the areas most affected were in Belarus, the Ukraine and Western Russia. An OECD Report notes that Chernobyl 'has serious and radiological, health and socio-economic consequences for the populations of Belarus, Ukraine and Russia, which still suffer from these consequences'.[6]

Initially, the Soviet authorities tried to cover up the incident. Many believe that, in the intervening years, there has been an attempt to downgrade the seriousness of the catastrophe. A World Health Organisation (WHO) report in 2005, based on work by other UN agencies, estimated that only 50 died and another 9,000 may die in the future as a result of being exposed to radiation. This presented the outcome of the accident in a much more favourable light. But it seemed to contradict many other reports and the experience of many people on the ground. The environ-

---

4. John Vidal, 'Hell on Earth', *The Guardian, Society/Guardian/ Environment,* 26 April 2006, page 9.
5. Seán McCárthaigh, 'An Explosive Subject', *The Irish Examiner,* 1 May 2006, page 4.
6. International Atomic Energy Agency, 2002, 'Chernobyl : Assessment of Radiological and Health Impacts: 2002 Update of Chernobyl: Ten Years On'. www.nea.fr/html/rp/chernobyl/chernobyl.html>

mental agency Greenpeace commissioned a response from 52 scientists who reviewed published data on Chernobyl. It estimated that 93,000 people have succumbed to terminal cancer and that the figure will rise to 100,000 in time. Even this is considered a conservative estimate by the Russian Academy of Medical Sciences which published a report claiming that 212,000 have died as a direct consequence of Chernobyl.[7]

Those most at risk were the more than 100,000 soldiers known as 'liquidators' who were brought in from all over the then Soviet Union to put out the fire and deal with the aftermath. This involved demolishing villages, dumping high levels of radioactive waste, cleaning railway lines and roads and decontaminating the environment. Many of these men developed terminal cancer but since they had returned to their communities they were often not counted among the casualties of Chernobyl. The children born to the liquidators are also dying at a younger age from a variety of cancers and many are also suffering from genetic defects and are malformed at birth. This is the real difference between accidents at nuclear facilities and accidents at other power plants.[8]

Dr Edward Walsh, writing in *The Irish Times*, claims that nuclear energy is 'the safest of all'. He opted for the WHO figure of 9,000 who have died as a result of the accident. He goes on to point to the 8,000 people who have lost their lives when hydroelectric dams burst. There is no denying this, but if one visits the site of the French Malpasset dam, one will not find the children of those who were killed there suffering from cancers or other deformities. People in the Malpasset area will be able to eat the food which is grown there. Not so with Chernobyl.[9] This is why for *The Guardian* reporter, John Vidal, Chernobyl is 'Hell on Earth' twenty years after the explosion. The failure of hydro-dams does not cause mutations in 18 generations of birds nor leave radiation levels in trees constantly rising.

7. John Vidal, 'Hell on Earth', op. cit., page 9.
8. ibid.
9. Edward Walsh, 'Nuclear energy 'the safest of all'', *The Irish Times*, 26 April 2006, page 16.

The Soviet Government is not the only government that has lied about nuclear accidents. Governments worldwide have consistently misled the public with regard to the dangers of nuclear power. It took the British authorities over thirty years to tell the full truth about the accident in Windscale in 1957. Two Irish research scientists, Dr Irene Hillary and Dr Patricia Sheehan have always believed that the unusually high incidences of cancer and Down's Syndrome in the Dundalk area of County Louth were related to the 1957 discharge of radioactive material from Windscale. Six girls out of a class of eleven gave birth to Down's Syndrome babies.[10]

It took the US government thirty-seven years to reveal that radioactive iodine had been discharged at the Hanford Nuclear Reservation in Washington State. The reservation encompasses 560 square miles of land in the Columbia River Basin. There are still many concerns about the health risks of nuclear power plants. In 1979, the largest radioactive spill in US history took place at the United Nuclear Mill at Church Rock, New Mexico. 100 million gallons of radioactive material contaminated the drinking water for over 1,700 Navajo people and their livestock. In the aftermath of the accident, the company refused to supply emergency food and water for the people who were affected by the spill. Rather than seeking to clear up the mess and minimise the damage, the company stonewalled for nearly five years before agreeing to pay a paltry $525,000 out of court settlement to the victims.[11] In March 2006, the State of Illinois filed a lawsuit against Exelon, the company which operates the Braidwood nuclear power station in Illinois, seeking damages over tritium leaks at the power plant.[12]

In May 2006, the British government brought a criminal prosecution against British Nuclear Group (BNG) which is a sub-

10. *The Irish Times*, 24 July 1984.
11. Frank Pitman, 'Navajos – UNC Settle Tailings-Spill Lawsuit', *Nuclear Fuels*, 22 Apri 1985.
12. Michael Brooks, 'Is it all over for nuclear?', *NewScientist*, 22 April 2006, page 37.

sidiary of British Nuclear Fuels in relation to a major leak in 2005 at the Thorp reprocessing plant. Under their licence the operators of Thorp, which is part of the Sellafield complex, are legally required to ensure that radioactive material is properly contained and if something happens, for example a major leak, they are required to report the matter to the relevant authorities. In this case, 83,000 litres of highly radioactive waste leaked from a pipe into a containment chamber. The waste contained 20 tonnes of uranium and plutonium. What is alarming about this is that staff did not notice the spill for at least eight months. The leak was reported in April 2005 even though it began probably in August 2004. It seems that the staff dismissed the leak as a technical glitch in March 2005 because of the large volume of the spill. An investigation found that there was operational complacency among the staff because of their belief that leaks at the plant were impossible because of the design of the operation, despite previous evidence to the contrary.[13] There were two other serious incidents at Sellafield in 2004. In one of these incidents three staff members were contaminated while carrying out maintenance work.[14]

Since 1997, there have been 57 incidents at existing nuclear plants. These incidents have included radiation leaks and machinery failure, contamination of ground water, employees' clothes and even a fire. On the international nuclear measurement scale, 11 of these incidents were deemed serious.[15] In July 2006, government nuclear inspectors raised serious questions about the safety of Britain's ageing nuclear power stations. Some of these installations have developed major cracks in their reactor cores and the company operating the plants do not know the extent of the damage or why it is taking place in the first instance.[16]

13. Liam Reid, 'Sellafield operators sued over major leak at processing plant', *The Irish Times*, 4 May 2006, page 8.
14. Sam Jones, 'Tally of mishaps hits Blair's nuclear hopes', *The Guardian*, 19 May 2006, page 4.
15. ibid.
16. John Vidal and Ian Sample, 'Unexplained cracks in reactor cores in-

Japan's nuclear industry has also been plagued by accidents, plant closures, major cost overruns and radiological releases which have led to the deaths of workers at nuclear facilities. In December 1995, when a sodium coolant leaked from the Fast Breeder Reactor in Monju, the nuclear industry attempted to cover up the full extent of the damage. This and other incidents have led to an erosion of public confidence in the industry which, as we will see later, has benefited the solar energy business.

The champions of nuclear power now use the connection between burning fossil fuel and global warming as a way of rehabilitating the nuclear power industry. The argument runs like this: unless countries build more nuclear power stations carbon dioxide emissions will continue to rise and countries will be unable to fulfill their commitments under the Kyoto Protocol. In addition everyone will suffer because of drastic climate change. This is why the British government commissioned an energy review in February 2006 which many believe will recommend building more nuclear power stations.

*Is nuclear energy green?*
We must ask ourselves is the above argument sound and is nuclear power really 'green'? If one looks merely at the nuclear plant itself, then it is true that very little fossil fuel is used to produce electricity. But the nuclear cycle from beginning to end is a much more extensive operation than what happens in the nuclear plant. An enormous quantity of fossil fuel is needed at almost every phase of the nuclear process which begins with uranium mining.

Mining uranium has very significant negative environmental consequences. The Olympic Dam uranium/copper mine in South Australia has produced a radioactive tailings dump of 60 million tonnes and it is increasing at 10 million tonnes each year. There are also major problems with water extraction because the

crease likelihood of accidents, says government inspectors', *The Guardian*, 5 July 2006, pages 1 and 2.

mine sucks more than 30 million litres of water from the Great
Artesian Basin. It is impossible to really quantify the full environmental cost of the operation since the mine has secured a
range of exemptions from environmental legislation. For example, it is exempt from the South Australian Environmental
Protection Act, The Water Resources Act, the Aboriginal
Heritage Act and the Freedom of Information Act.[17] Little wonder that the 2003 Senate's Inquiry into the regulation of uranium
mining in Australia found 'a pattern of underperformance and
non-compliance'. It went on to identify 'many gaps in knowledge and found an absence of reliable data on which to measure
the extent of contamination or its impact on the environment'. It
concluded that changes were required 'in order to protect the
environment and its inhabitants from serious or irreversible
damage'.[18] The mine is also the largest consumer of electricity in
South Australia making it the state's major contributor to global
warming.

Most deposits of uranium are at a concentration of 0.01-0.02.
These are found in Australia, Canada, South Africa, Russia, US
and Kazakhstan. Typically 98,000 tonnes of rock has to be mined
and milled in order to produce a single tonne of uranium. A typical 100mv/er nuclear reactor will require in the region of 160
tonnes of uranium each year.[19] Milling uses huge diesel-pow-
ered machines to crush the rock. Then sulphuric acid is used to
leach uranium from the rock. Other elements are also leached,
among them molybdemiun, selenium, arsenic and lead. These
are removed before the fully milled product is completed which

17. Australian Conservation Foundation, 2005, Submission to Standing
Committee on Industry and Resources, Inquiry into Developing
Australia's Non-fossil Fuel Energy Industry. www.aph.gov.au/
house/committee/isr/uranium.subs.html>
18. Senate Environment, Communications, Information Technology
and the Arts Reference and Legislation Committee, October 2003,
Regulating the Ranger, Jabiluka, Berverly and Honeymoon uranium
mines', www.aph.gov.au/senate/committee/ecita_ctee /completed_
inquiry/2002-04/uranium/report/index.htm>
19. Jon Hughes, 'Uranium mining and milling', The Ecologist, July-
August 2006, page 4.

is called yellowcake. The yellowcake is packed in drums and sent to the nuclear facility. This, of course, involves major security risks as the yellowcake can be used to make primitive, but lethal nuclear weapons. The tailings from the milling, much of which contains uranium, have now to be secured and dealt with. This often does not happen. In the 1980s, material which contained highly radioactive tailings was used to build houses.[20]

Beyond milling there is the process of enrichment which is not unlike distillation. The problem with this process is that the yellowcake only contains 0.7% uranium-235. This is the major ingredient in nuclear fission. To increase the concentration of uranium -235 to 3.5%, the oxide is mixed with fluorine and heated to form uranium hexafluoride gas which is often called 'hex'. In this process the lighter molecules of uranium-235 are separated from the uranium 238 by straining the compound through a membrane with a number of small openings. During the cooling process the uranium returns to a solid state and is then ready for conversion into fuel rods.

At every stage of the nuclear journey there is nuclear waste. The further one moves along the journey the more toxic and radioactive the waste becomes. 85% of the material used in the enrichment process is also waste and is known as depleted uranium. This is toxic and highly carcinogenic and has to be placed and stored in sealed containers until it can be safely dealt with, presumably by placing it in a safe geological site. For many reasons, which include cost and the opposition of local people, suitable places have not been found thus far. In the US alone, there now is 500,000 tonnes of depleted uranium in storage. Some of the gases used in the enrichment process are also toxic and contribute hugely to global warming. For example, fluorine and its halogenated compounds have 10,000 times more global warming capacity than carbon dioxide. The nuclear industry does not keep records of the quantity of the various forms of fluorine re-

20. Jon Hughes, ibid, page 045.

leased into the atmosphere.[21] Enriching the uranium also uses enormous amounts of fossil fuel. In the 1970s, in the US alone seven 1,000 megawatt coal-fired plants were used to enrich uranium.

Much of the uranium mined in Australia is destined for Japan. The nuclear industry in Japan has a poor record in terms of safety. A number of serious accidents have taken place in recent years as well as the systematic falsification of safety data.[22] There is also concern that Japan's plutonium research programme will enable it to develop nuclear weapons if the need arises. Given the new tensions that are already evident in Asia with the growth of the Chinese economy, if Japan opts to become a new nuclear power it could create all kinds of geopolitical problems.

A huge amount of fossil fuel is used in the building of nuclear power plants and reinforcing the reactor to safeguard it against accidents. It is estimated that building each reactor produces 20 million tonnes of carbon dioxide. As the Oxford Research Group writes, 'Given that one of the main factors (in promoting nuclear energy) is the amount of carbon dioxide produced by the mining and milling of uranium ore, the use of the poorer ores in nuclear reactors would produce more carbon dioxide emission than burning fossil fuels directly, and may actually consume more electricity than it produces.'[23] Reactors also need 30 million gallons of water per day to stop generators overheating.[24]

If one adds up these three phases of the nuclear process it is estimated that a reactor would have to operate continuously for over 10 years before producing a net unit of energy. But the fossil fuel used in the nuclear operation does not stop when electricity generated by nuclear power plants reaches the national

21. Jon Hughes, 'Conversion and Enrichment', The Ecologist, July–August, 2006, page 47.
22. Shaun Burnie and Aileen Mioko Smith, 'Japan's nuclear twilight zone', Bulletin of the Atomic Scientists, Vol 57, No 03, May/June 2001, pp 58-62, www.thebulletin.org/article.php?art_ofn=mj01burnie>
23. Chris Abbot, Paul Rogers and John Sloboda, op. cit., 12
24. John Hughes, 'Building a Nuclear Power Station', The Ecologist, July-August, 2006, page 42.

grid. At the end of their 30 or 40 years lifespan, vast amounts of fossil fuel will be needed to decommission nuclear plants. Decommissioning will not be cheap. In 1993, Sir John Bourn, head of the National Audit Office in Britain, told the members of Parliament that the total cost of decommissioning and reprocessing was a financial time bomb. He estimated that it could run as high as £40 billion.[25] That figure has now jumped to £70 billion, which means that the nuclear industry has been the greatest loss making industry in British history.[26] Interestingly, it is a small group of US companies like Fluor and Bechtel who are poised to secure the contract for the proposed nuclear clean-up which could last anything up to 75 years, especially the huge and complex site at Sellafield. There are 20 million cubic metres of contaminated land at the 770 acre site.[27]

Unfortunately, even a rehabilitated, greenfield site does not lay to rest the nuclear genie. Fossil fuels will be needed to transport and store nuclear waste for umpteen generations. Strontium 90, for example, is radioactive for 600 years. This time span is only a flick of an eyelid when compared to plutonium. This is the most significant element in the nuclear waste cocktail and it is radioactive for over a quarter of a million years. Plutonium is so lethal that a few kilos spread evenly around the world would cause a massive epidemic of cancer. At present, Britain has 10,000 tonnes of intermediate and high-level nuclear waste. The Department of Trade and Industry in Britain has estimated that this will increase 50-fold by the end of the century even if no new nuclear facilities are built.[28]

The Intergovernmental Panel on Climate Change (IPCC) has estimated that if there were a 10-fold increase in nuclear power

25. 'Nuclear Shut-Down Is a Financial Time Bomb', *The Ecologist*, January/February 1998, pp 9 -14.
26. Michael Meacher, 'Returning to nuclear power could prove a deadly U-turn', *The Guardian*, Society/Guardian/Environment, 1 February 2006.
27. Terry, Macalister, 'American engineers in line for jobs until 2080 on Britain's nuclear clean-up', *The Guardian*, 15 February 2006, page 2 of 3
28. Michael Meacher, 'Returning to nuclear power could prove a deadly U-Turn', op.cit., page 8.

generation in the 21st century, this would produce a stockpile of between 50,000 and 100,000 tonnes of plutonium. The response of the IPCC is that the security risk 'would be colossal'.[29] Each 1000 megawatt nuclear reactor produces about 30 metric tonnes of high level of radioactive waste each year.[30]

*Nuclear Power is not cheap*

Nuclear power is not cheap. The last British nuclear power station, Sizewell B, was built in Suffok in 1995. The price paid by the taxpayer then was £2.733 billion which would translate into £3.7 billion in 2005 figures. It took 15 years to complete and cost twice the original budget. If commercial companies had built the plant the cost of borrowing the money would have pushed the total over the £4 billion mark. It would take more than six similar nuclear power plants to supply 20% of Britain's electricity. Both land based and off-shore windfarms would supply the same amount of energy for a similar cost of around £25 billion according to Dr Dave Toke.[31] At that point the cost bias moves in favour of wind energy as fuel costs are free and decommissioning is much, much less expensive. Walt Patterson, an associate fellow in the energy, environment and development programme at Chatham House, makes the point that for tackling climate change or insuring security of supply, nuclear energy is the 'slowest, most expensive, least flexible and riskiest option'.[32]

The former environment minister Michael Meacher believes

29. Intergovernmental Panel on Climate Change, 1995, 'Climate Change 1995: Impacts, Adaptations and Mitigation of Climate Change: Scientific-Technical Analyses', Contribution of Working Group 11 to the Second Assessment of the Intergovernmental Panel on Climate Change, R.T. Watson, M.C. Zinyowera, R.H. Moss (eds), Cambridge University Press, UK. See also Greenpeace, 'Nuclear Energy: No Solution to Climate Change', www.archive.greenpeace.org/comms/ no.nukes/nenstcc.html>

30 Jon Hughes, 'Nuclear waste', *The Ecologist*, July-August 2006, page 55.

31. Dave Toke, 'Doubters; 'It strains the logic of energy', *The Guardian*, *Society/Guardian/Environment*, 5 October 2005, page 9.

32. Walt Patterson, 'Time for an upgrade', *The Guardian*, 17 May 2006, *Society/Guardian/Environment*, page 8.

that, given the costs and the risks, the private sector would not invest in nuclear facilities unless the government underwrites the loans and provides tax relief for the industry.[33] This will be difficult to do in the present European economic climate. Adris Piebalgs, the Commissioner for Energy in the European Commission, wants to see different forms of energy compete against each other on a level playing field and will not countenance the use of state funds to subsidise nuclear power.[34]

If economics is undermining the viability of building new nuclear power stations, the time it takes to build one may be a further nail in the coffin of the industry. The only nuclear power plant at present being built in Europe is at Oikiluoto in Finland. This is a relatively new design which is schedule to be completed in 2009. There is simply not the capacity to start a massive nuclear building programme in Britain or around the world. In October 2005, Ian Fells, an energy consultant told an energy conference at Rimini in Italy that there are only six building corporations in the world capable of building nuclear power stations. None of these companies were British and the specialised personnel who built the last British nuclear plant Sizewell B are either retired or dead.[35] Even to retain the present nuclear *status quo* in Britain would now require the building of eight to ten nuclear power stations which have no hope of being completed and operational before 2025.

Other rich countries face similar problems. Australia is probably unique in that between 85 and 90 per cent of its electricity is generated by coal-fired plants. This adds hugely to Australia's greenhouse gas emissions. In April 2006, Peter Costello, the Federal Treasurer, warned Australians that they would need to develop a domestic nuclear power industry as part of the solution to global warming. Dr Iain McGill, research co-ordinator for

---

33. David Toke, op. cit.
34. Michael Brooks 'Is it all over for nuclear power?', *New Scientist*, 22 April 2006, page 36.
35. Idem 37.

the Centre for Energy and Environmental Markets at the University of New South Wales responded to the Treasurer by pointing out that it would take between 40 and 50, 1000-megawatt nuclear power plants to substitute for the coal-fired ones. Realistically, such a programme would take decades to achieve.

Dr Mark Diesendorf, another scientist at the Institute of Environmental Studies at the same university, also pointed out how costly in economic, environmental and social terms such a venture would be. According to him, a 1000 megawatt nuclear plant would cost at least $A3 billion to build which is two-and-a-half times that of a coal-fired plant. To embark on such a massive building programme over 20 years, would add significantly to Australia's greenhouse gas emissions. He believes that it would take 40 years to break even in terms of carbon dioxide emissions. You would have a big spike in carbon dioxide emissions … 'I think the whole thing is insane,' he said of the suggestion that nuclear power could help fight global warming.[36]

Even without factoring in the decommissioning costs, alternative energies like wind are now almost as cheap as nuclear power. While the nuclear industry claims that nuclear power can produce a kilowatt hour of electricity for 3 pence, this is disputed by other sources. A 2005 report from a London-based think-tank called the New Economics Foundation estimated that the cost of a kilowatt-hour of electricity generated from a nuclear power source would cost 8.3 pence once realistic construction and running costs are included. The UK Royal Academy of Engineers put the cost of a kilowatt hour of electricity generated from gas at 3.4 pence, 5 pence for coal and 7.2 pence for wind.[37]

Despite that fact that Prime Minister Tony Blair put rebuilding nuclear plants back on the agenda in May 2006, many people believe that economic arguments will scuttle the proposal to

36. Wendy Frew, 'Nuclear no cure for climate change, scientist warn', *The Sydney Morning Herald*, 2 May 2006, www.smh.com.au/news/national/nuclear no-cure-for-climate-change/2006/05/02.
37. Michael Brooks, 'Is it all over for nuclear power? *The New Scientist*, 22 April 2006, page 6.

build new nuclear power plants. According to Tom Burke, a visiting professor at both Imperial College, London and University College, London, 'nuclear power stations are financially risky projects. You spend hundreds of millions of pounds for at least a decade before you start to recover any earnings. Since you have to pay for the financing, as well as the direct construction costs, this makes nuclear power much less attractive to investors than any other form of electricity generation.'[38] The only way to make the nuclear option palatable to investors is to push up the price of electricity. The public will hardly tolerate such an action.

The proponents of nuclear power often forget to tell us that the supply of uranium is also finite. Many believe that the supply of uranium peaked as far back as 1981. According to Michael Meacher, the gap is now being filled by using uranium from the military stockpile. This source is predicted to end around 2013. The nuclear industry is attempting to find new mines in Canada, Australia and Kazakhstan. Developing a nuclear mine is difficult and expensive. Meacher reckons that it takes 15 years to bring a mine to production from the time it is discovered. But even with new mines on line, the supply will fill only half of the accessible gap for the 440 nuclear plants which are currently producing power. With 20 new nuclear stations under construction around the world and another 30 new plants in China, the problem of access to uranium will become a major problem. Meacher believes that one quarter of nuclear power plants might be forced to close down because of a lack of fuel.[39] He also points out that the cost of uranium has increased by 400% in the past 6 years. Charles Kernot, a mining analyst at Seymour Pearce in London, shares Meacher's view on the scarcity of uranium. He believes that 'there is a great expectation that there is not going to be enough uranium to feed the new nuclear power stations being built all over the world and that is what has

---

38. Tom Burke, 'Nuclear industry will only build stations the prime minister wants if he forces up electricity prices', *The Guardian*, 18 May 2006, page 34.
39. Meacher, Michael, 'On the Road to Ruin', *The Guardian*, *Society/Guardian/Environment*, 7 June 2006, page 8.

driven the price up'.[40] Only a few countries produce uranium. Canada is the leader with an annual output of 11, 800 tonnes, followed by Australia at 7,900 tonnes and Kazakhstan produces 4,300 tonnes.[41]

When challenged about dwindling uranium supplies, the nuclear industry claims that the element thorium can be used instead of uranium. Meacher points out that Japan, Russia, Germany, India and the US have been studying thorium reactors for 30 years and as yet no commercial thorium reactor has been built. Given this immanent uranium shortage it is the height of folly to invest in new nuclear installations which will cost at least £3 billion each (and possibly more), particularly if one quarter of them will be forced to shut down because of lack of fuel.[42]

Another reason that questions should be raised about the claim that nuclear power will help us win the battle against global warming is that nuclear power is used merely to generate electricity. Generating electricity is only responsible for one third of greenhouse gas emissions. Even if there was a doubling of nuclear power output by the year 2050 this would only reduce greenhouse gas emissions by a mere 5%. This is less that one tenth of what the scientists at the Intergovernmental Panel on Climate Change (IPCC) are asking for in order to stabilise the climate.

*Nuclear Power and September 11th 2001*
The events of 11 September 2001 have changed many facets of our lives. Nuclear power stations are now being seen as potential terrorist targets. Security reasons alone should lead to their demise. A study conducted by the Union of Concerned Scientists came to the conclusion that a major terrorist attack on a major nuclear power installation, like the Indian Point reactor on the

---

40. Terry Macalister, 'Prince of uranium soars', *The Guardian*, 18 May 2006, page 7.
41. ibid.
42. ibid.

Hudson River in the US, could result in over 40,000 deaths in the short run from acute radiation syndrome and in the long-term over 500,000 from cancer among people within a 50 mile radius of the plant.[43] Experts are worried that the new Pressurised Water Reactor (EPR) being built at Oikiluoto in Finland is vulnerable from the point of view of a terrorist attack. A French report prepared by the power company Électricité de France for the French nuclear safety regulator (IRSN) was leaked to the press. The report stated that the reactor could withstand an attack from a 5 tonne military fighter jet. Greenpeace commissioned a response from an independent nuclear expert, John Large. He found that such an attack would be a total calamity and would release large quantities of radioactive material into the surrounding environment.[44]

The International Atomic Energy Agency has a data base which attempts to track efforts to smuggle radioactive material or yellowcake. There are 650 confirmed incidents and 100 of these incidents took place in 2004.[45] Such activities provide fissile material for nuclear weapons or other radioactive material for making 'dirty bombs'. In February 2006, the EU Commission criticised Sellafield directors and staff for the way in which they account for their nuclear material.[46] In another instance, undercover US Congressional investigators successfully smuggled enough radio active material into the US to make two dirty bombs, even after alarms were set off on radiation detectors which had been installed at border checkpoints. Dirty bombs can force long-term evacuation of people by spreading low levels

43. Edwin S. Lyman, September 2004, 'Chernobyl on the Hudson? The Health and Economic Impacts of a Terrorist Attack at the Indian Point Nuclear Plant.'www.ucsusa.org/global_security/nuclear_ terrorism/page.cfm?page1D=1508>

44. Nuclear 9/11?, *NewScientist*, 27, 2006, page 6.

45. Mohamed El Baradel, 2005, 'Nuclear Terrorism: Identifying and Combating the Risks', Statement of Director General of the IAEA, 16 March 2005. www.iaea.org/News Center/Statements/ 2005/ebsp2005 n003.html>

46. www.business.guardian.co.uk/16/02/2006

of radioactivity across an area after being detonated with a conventional explosive.[47] Given the highly unstable political situation internationally, it is foolish in the extreme to allow this material to fall into the hands of terrorists for their lethal use.

*Transporting Nuclear Waste*
Moving nuclear waste around a country like Britain produces
carbon emissions and is another potential area where serious accidents can occur. In fact there are thirty accidents involving
nuclear trains each year in Britain. Some are not too serious but
the derailment of a train carrying nuclear waste near the Hinkley
Point power station in Somerset in 2003 led Prime Minister Blair
to promise a comprehensive safety review of nuclear cargo.
Critics dismiss the subsequent report as merely a list of the year's
events without even proposing a single recommendation.

Greenpeace asked the nuclear consultant John Large to examine the whole scenario of transporting nuclear waste on
trains. The waste is stored in 30cm-thick forged steel flasks
which have been rigorously fire tested and drop tested. Even so,
John Large makes the point that these flasks would not withstand a typical train tunnel fire where temperatures can reach
1000 degrees celsius. In such an eventuality, water would be
forced out of the flasks and the fuel inside would ignite. The
subsequent radiation could be spread over six kilometres and
kill and maim many people, resulting in a legacy of cancers and
other diseases in the area for decades. At this moment in time,
thousands of tonnes of nuclear waste and are being moved
across many countries and through densely populated cities like
London. The pro-nuclear lobby believes that no accident, under
any circumstances, can happen. This is a dangerous position to
take in a fallible and imperfect world where human error is always a risk with something as deadly as nuclear waste.[48]

---

47. Eric Lipton, 'Testers Slip Radioactive Materials Over Borders', *New York Times*, 28 March 2006. www.nytimes/march 28, 2006
48. Madeleine Brettingham, 'Tracking hazard', *The Guardian, Society/ Guardian/ Environment*, 31 May 2006, page 8.

Finally, the most compelling reason for not proceeding with nuclear power is that the waste is so toxic and we do not know what to do with it. A run of the mill power plant produces 25-30 tonnes of spent fuel each year. Given the number of nuclear plants worldwide, this means that 12,000-14,000 tonnes of spent fuel are produced by the industry annually. Without any long-term solution for dealing with nuclear waste, the stocks continue to pile up.

Reprocessing nuclear waste has its own inherent problems because highly radioactive waste material has to be carried over long distances using fossil fuel. Though there are still thousands of tonnes to be dealt with, not a single country has yet secured a long-term repository for dumping high level radioactive waste. Potential sites have been identified in only a few countries such as the US, Sweden and Finland. At present the limits which are being proposed for the radioactive dump at Yucca Mountain in the US mean that this dump, when it is built, will not be able to deal with the current output of radioactive waste from existing nuclear plants. If the nuclear industry were to expand significantly it would be necessary to build a facility like the one at Yucca Mountain every three or four years.[49] The chance of this happening are very slim indeed.

In March 2006, the Sustainable Development Commission (SDC) did a detailed study on whether Britain should restart a nuclear power programme as a way of solving the current energy crisis. The SDC conducted eight detailed studies covering such areas as safety, economics and how to deal with nuclear waste. They weighed up the pros and cons and came down firmly against nuclear energy. The Commission suggested an 'aggressive' expansion of energy efficiency, in addition to the promoting of alternative, green energy. The SDC reminded the public that even if the UK's current nuclear capacity was doubled, it would only lead to an 8% drop in carbon dioxide emissions by the year 2035.[50]

49. Stephen Ansolabehere et al, 'The Future of Nuclear Power: An Interdisciplinary MIT Study', 2003. www.web.mit.edu/nuclearpower>
50. 'A nuclear 'no', *The New Scientist*, 11 March 2006, page 7.

*The Vatican should not support Nuclear Power*

For the above reasons I hope that the Vatican, which in other spheres preaches a pro-life ethic, will now stop endorsing this death-dealing technology. Since the successful campaign in the early 1980s to stop a nuclear power plant in Bataan near Manila in the Philippines, I have been critical of the Vatican's support for nuclear power. At the International Atomic Agency (IAEA) in Vienna in September 1982, Mgr Mario Peressin, the Vatican representative at IAEA at the time stated that 'the use of nuclear power did, however, involve risks associated either with accidents that might arise at nuclear power stations or with the storage of radioactive waste. Certain groups of naïve idealists and even certain personalities from the scientific, political, cultural or religious worlds condemned the use of nuclear power simply for that reason.'

A decade later, Archbishop Donato Squiccianrini went even further in his address to IAEA. He stated that 'the Holy See believes that all possible efforts should be made to extend to all countries, especially to developing ones, the benefits contained in the peaceful use of nuclear power.'

Finally, at a seminar in Rome organised by the Pontifical Academy of the Sciences and the Ukrainian Embassy to the Holy See, the president of the Pontifical Council for Justice and Peace, Cardinal Renato Martino invited the international community to support the development of nuclear energy for civilian use. He confirmed the Holy See's interest in 'the continuing research on nuclear energy for civilian ends, so rich in technical, cultural and political applications'. He continued to articulate the Vatican's dismissive attitude towards those who are opposed to nuclear power by stating that 'the seminar has taught us that nuclear energy must not be seen, as it often is, through the spectacles of ideological prejudice but with the look of intelligence, human rationality and science, accompanied by the wise exercise of prudence, in view of carrying out the integral and solidaristic development of the human person and nation.'[51]

51. www.zenit.org 'Holy See Backs Civil Use of Nuclear Energy,' Vatican City, 27 April 2006.

*The Pro-Nuclear Propaganda*

The Cardinal seems to be unaware of the amount of money which the nuclear industry has used to promote their industry. Information obtained through the freedom of information (FOI) legislation reveals that Nirex, the body responsible for finding solutions for nuclear waste in Britain, has spent £1 million of tax-payers' money on PR since 2003. One of the groups targeted by Nirex was 'Parliament and Government'. They set about using the old PR tactic 'divide and rule' to win over MPs. So the strategy for Nirex was firstly to bolster and if possible enlist those MPs who support their policy. Secondly, to convince those MPs who were indifferent or undecided to back nuclear power and finally to isolate and try to convince those MPs who are against their policy.[52]

But Nirex are really only small players in this campaign. It is hardly surprising that British Nuclear Fuels (BNFL) are in the forefront of the pro-nuclear campaign. Once again information obtained under the freedom of information legislation (FOI) reveals that BNFL provides information cards known as 'race-cards' to promote nuclear power. These cards suggest that the debate is to be kept 'personal' and 'simple' to emphasise that nuclear power protects 'values'. They also denigrate other forms of energy, especially renewables. In October 2005, a Strategic Awareness Document claims that 'without nuclear power, renewables will not make a difference. Nuclear provides 'always on' electricity. Renewable energy is, by its nature intermittent.' This document also addresses and dismisses safety considerations. 'Everyday emissions into the air are safe. More in a bottle of mineral water – excellent.'[53]

The pro-nuclear message does not stop with promotional briefings for their staff. Philip Dewhurst is the public affairs director of BNFL. He is a former president of the Institute of Public Relations. In an interview with *PR Week* (a trade magazine of the

---

52. www.nuclearspin.org/nirex/targeted groups, May 3, 2006>
53. Andy Rowell, 'Plugging the gap', *The Guardian*, *Society/Guardian/Environment*, 3 May 2006, page 9.

industry), he said that BNFL was promoting the nuclear option 'via third-party opinion because the public would be suspicious if we started ramming pro-nuclear messages down their throats.'[54] What a coup for the pro-nuclear industry to have the Vatican promoting their interests. They must be delighted to hear a cardinal in such an important office as President of the Pontifical Council for Justice and Peace attacking critics of this dangerous technology and accusing them of being blinded by 'ideological prejudice'. How ironic for a pro-life church.

*Future Possibilities with Fusion*

Some scientists believe that nuclear fusion – the energy that powers the sun – will provide plenty of affordable energy within the next 50 years. In contrast to nuclear fission, which tears atomic nuclei apart in order to produce energy, fusion squeezes the nuclei of two hydrogen atoms together. It does this by heating a plasma of hydrogen isotopes to 100 million degrees celsius which is 10 times hotter than the sun. The process releases a helium nucleus, a neutron and huge quantities of energy. The resulting hydrogen fuel is partly heavy hydrogen or deuterium. This can be readily extracted from the water molecule as part-heavy hydrogen or tritium. Deuterium can also be made from lithium which is a metal that is found in many parts of the world.

There is one major problem with fusion, which may have been solved recently by US scientists. Because of the extreme temperature that is necessary for this process, the steel reactor vessel can be damaged by plasma instabilities called edge-localised modes (ELMs). The physicist Kurt Kleiner explains this with an analogy; he compares it 'to a balloon bulging between fingers that are squeezing it. (The) hot plasma occasionally flares out of the magnetic field and (this) corrodes the inside of the vessel.'[55] US researchers have found a way to bleed some of the plasma particles from the field's edge. This prevents plasma

54. ibid.
55. Kurt Kiener, 'How to protect fusion reactors from flare-ups', *New Scientist*, 27 May 2006, page 11.

bursting out in ELMs and damaging the reactor vessel. Without this breakthrough, it would be necessary to replace the reactor vessel every six months which could cost hundreds of millions of euro.

Fusion could potentially produce an enormous amount of energy. It is estimated that from the amount of lithium in a single laptop computer, plus the heavy hydrogen in half a bath tub of water, these could provide energy enough for an average European for thirty years. Fusion is much safer that fission. Nuclear meltdown would be almost impossible. All that would be necessary to stop the process would be to turn off the magnetic jackets that keep the fuel in the reactor. There is also much less fuel involved. At Jet in Oxfordshire there exists an experimental fusion reactor. The amount of fuel being used there is a mere gram in contrast to the 250 tonnes of uranium which was present at Chernobyl.

The main problem with fusion is that harnessing the energy has proved extremely difficult. Research into fusion began in the 1950s. Even then there were those who claimed that it would provide substantial amounts of energy before the end of the 20th century. The fundamental problem is how to get the two hydrogen nuclei close enough to fuse and how to control the reaction. It takes an enormous amount of energy to change even a gram of fusion fuel into a super-hot gas or plasma.

This feat was achieved for the first time at the fusion reactor at Jet in Oxfordshire. The problem was that it was not viable in energy terms. While the fusion worked, the reaction which was created only released 70% of the energy which was demanded to start the fusion in the first place. In a commendable show of international solidarity the EU, Japan, China, South Korea, India and the US signed an agreement to build a fusion reactor called Iter in Cadarache in Southern France. This reactor will be 10 times bigger that the Jet reactor in Oxfordshire. The cost will be in the region of €10 billion. 33 scientists from Dublin City

University and 10 from University College Cork will take part in this venture.[56]

Supporters of fusion technology claim that fusion is the way of the future as it will address our energy needs without the downsides associated with nuclear fission. On the down side critics claim that governments are pouring a huge amount of money down the drain after a technology which will never deliver results.[57]

To return to the problems with fission, in *Greening the Christian Millennium* I reflected that in the wake of the accidents at Chernobyl, Three Mile Island and Sellafield, the nexus between nuclear weapons and the so-called peaceful use of nuclear power, plus the continuing problems of dealing with nuclear waste, people are justifiably fearful of nuclear power. The fears are real and I would like to see the Vatican take the matter much more seriously. I find it difficult to understand how Christians who believe that the earth was created and is sustained by God, can support a form of energy that is inherently dangerous and will remain lethal for tens of thousands years.[58]

56. Aine Kerr, 'Irish scientists to assist in €10bn 'safe' nuclear energy project', *The Irish Times*, 25 May 2006, page10.
57. James Randerson, 'When the dream of harnessing the sun's power could come true', *The Guardian*, www.guardian.co.uk/print24/05/2006
58. Seán McDonagh, 1999, *Greening the Christian Millennium*, Dominican Publications, Dublin, page 118.

# CHAPTER 7

# Energy Efficiency and Renewables

Every effort ought to be made to reduce our energy needs and to promote and support alternative, non-polluting sources of energy. However, we should not fool ourselves into thinking that alternative energy sources will allow us to continue expanding our energy needs without doing irreparable damage to the planetary systems which sustain all life on earth. No combination of alternatives will substitute for the 82.5 million barrels of oil that the world consumed every day in 2005.

Nevertheless, it is true that are huge possibilities for achieving energy savings. A report in February 2006 by the California-based Electric Power Research Institute found that a two track approach can yield significant savings. These include implementing energy efficient initiatives and developing technologies which more accurately respond to demand. Michael Brooks points to a US company which built gas-fuelled power plants which were capable of generating 200 gigawatts of electricity. However, the anticipated demand never arose so that the investors lost $100 billion.[1]

Businesses are saving money by cutting energy imputs. Johnson & Johnson decided in the late 1990s to voluntarily meet Kyoto targets. In the period 1990 to 2005, the company reduced carbon emissions by 11.5%. During that period sales grew by 350%.[2] A DuPont operation at Chambers Works in New Jersey has seen a one-third reduction in energy use per kilogram of chemical product. Toyota US has reduced its energy use per unit

---

1. Michael Brooks, op. cit., page 35.
2. Jad Mouawad, 'The Greener Guys', *The New York Times*, www.nytimes.com/26/05/30/30carbon.html page 3 of 4.

of production by 15% from a 2000 base. In Malaysia, a factory making disk drives run by Western Digital has reduced energy use by 44%.

In Japan, energy consumption per person is half of what it is in the US. There are 11 million low emission vehicles, which is around 21% of the total fleet. Japanese steel making plants can produce one tonne of steel using 20% less electricity than their US counterparts and 50% less than in China. In the Tokyo region, – which is the world's largest urban area – 'intelligent machines' from subway ticketing machines to lifts, automatically turn off when not in use. The Japanese government has set strict standards for electronic instruments. Both home and office air conditioners must use 63% less power by 2008. Canon's Pixus printer is very energy efficient. It uses 60% less energy than any of the company's other models. It is now the number one bestseller in Japan, even though there are cheaper printers on the market.[3] Some commentators, like Amory Lovins of the Rocky Mountain Institute, a Colorado-based energy analysis firm, believe that we have only scratched the surface when it comes to using energy more effectively.[4]

Houses can be made much more energy-efficient. The 'super-window' can play a significant role in energy efficiency. It is based on the greenhouse effect of glass and glazing. In this case the glazing is coated with a special insulation film. It is then sealed and gases such as krypton or a silica foam are pumped into the space, thus providing excellent insulation because heat is trapped in the house. Other parts of the house, such as the attic and the walls, also need to be well insulated. The goal is to create a house which does not loose energy. Alan Simpson, MP for Nottingham South, argues that every household in the country should generate some of its own electricity. He believes that Britain's energy needs could be met twice over if it opted for a less centralised generating system. The solar panels on his own

3. Anthony Faiola, 'Turn off the heat – how Japan made energy savings an art form', *The Guardian*, 17 February 2006, page 24.
4. Michael Brooks, op.cit., 35 and 36.

house provide about 75% of his electricity needs. He emphasises the importance of good insulation. An enormous amount of heat is lost because of poor insulation. He reckons that 50% can escape through a poorly insulated roof and 20% though single gazed windows.[5]

Government support ought to be available so that every house or business premises built in the future is equipped with solar power. A green paper prepared for the European Commission claimed that energy efficiency could cut the consumption of electricity by 20% over 15 years. Such a strategy would save an estimated €60 billion in energy costs. The biggest saving would come from the building sector if proper procedures were followed to insulate houses. Unfortunately, over half a million houses which were built in Ireland since 1995 are not energy-efficient according to Frank McDonald, the environment editor of *The Irish Times*, 'because the government dithered for so long over changing the building regulations to impose higher insulation standards'.[6] The leader of the Green Party in Ireland, Trevor Sargent, claimed that documents released under the Freedom of Information legislation make it very clear that the Fianna Fáil led government took a decision to delay implementation of EU Energy Directive, aimed at improving the energy efficiency of buildings, so that it would not affect the concrete industry adversely.[7] The provisions in the EU Energy Performance of Buildings Directive stipulates that all buildings put on the market for sale or rent must have a Building Energy Rating (BER). This was supposed to come into effect on 1 January 2006 but under 'transitional arrangements' made by the Minister for the Environment, buildings for which planning permission was sought before 30 June 2006 are exempt, provided they are substantially completed by the end of June 2008.[8] The tragedy is that

5. Ben Willis, 'Energy Hero: Alan Simpson', *Ecologist*, June 2006, pages 58-62.
6. Frank McDonald, 'How a lot of hot air creates a legacy of cold houses', *The Irish Times*, 17 July 2006, page 6.
7. Paul O'Brien, 'Green man sees red', *The Irish Examiner*, 24 August 2006, page 17.
8. ibid.

houses which are expensive to buy will be expensive to heat in the future.

With rising energy prices, good insulation makes sound economic sense. It could cut €1,513 off the energy costs of the average household each year. Unfortunately, the pressure to reduce energy use has come, not from the Irish government but from the EU Commission. This reduction would also cut carbon dioxide emissions from the housing sector which averages out at eight tonnes for each of the 1.4 million households in Ireland each year.[9] Sustainable Energy Ireland (SEI) have produced a booklets on how to make one's home more energy efficient. The booklet illustrates how each room in the house from the attic through to the bathroom, bedrooms, kitchen, living room and dining room can all be made more energy efficient.[10] Research by (SEI) found that the efficiency in the whole electricity grid increased by 1% in 2004 to 41%.[11] This would indicate that there is quite a long way to go in promoting energy efficiency. Ireland is particularly vulnerable since 87% of our energy comes from imported fossil fuel sources.[12]

*Hydro-Power*

In the year 1998, it was estimated that 22% of the world's electricity is generated from a hydro source. Hydro-stations were one of the first ways of producing electricity in the later part of the 19th century and early 20th century. Many of these power stations are huge installations like the one at Ardnacrusha on the Shannon River, near Limerick. Very often water is dammed up into a reservoir so that there is a sufficient constant flow to drive

9. 'Switch off: ways to reduce the energy bill', *The Irish Times*, Weekend Review, 14 January 2006, page 2.
10. *How to Make Your Home More Energy Efficient*, Sustainable Energy Ireland, Glasnevin, Dublin 9.
11. *Energy in Ireland 1990 – 2004, Trends, issues, forecasts and indicators*, SEI Sustainable Energy Ireland, Energy Policy Statistical Support Unit, January 2006, page 2.
12. 'Call to leave fossils to the historians', *Irish Independent*, Special Report, 29 March 2006, page 15.

the turbines. Initially in the 1920s, Ardnacrusha was expected to meet all the electricity needs of the country. Today, because of huge rise in demand, it meets only 2% of peak hour demand.

There is not too much scope for developing large scale hydro in Ireland. So the future of hydro electricity would seem to be in small scale units of between 2.5 and 25 megawatts which do not involve impounding water. Even though the initial costs of building a hydro plant may be significant, one of the main advantages of hydro is the exceptionally long life of the installation and the low running costs. Hydro power is also almost instantaneous. During the black out that affected 50 million people in the eastern US and Canada in 2003, hydo stations were the first to be put into the grid to stabilise the system and restore power.[13] Another difficulty is that many governments and large scale utility companies prefer to build large power plants and develop a centralised grid. People who wish to install small scale hydro systems on rivers adjacent to their property often run into problems with the planning authorities. These authorities fear that installing a small scale hydro-plant on a river will interfere with other activities like boating and fishing. However, many of these concerns can be taken on board with proper design, planning and impact mitigation measures.

There are also difficulties about getting connections with the national grid. Because the technology involved in producing hydro-electricity has been around for a long time there is a perception that there is little room for further technical development. The truth is that there is plenty of scope for research and development in this area which will make small scale hydro more efficient and easy to install. One major step that needs to be taken to make this and other renewable energies attractive to producers and consumers is to clarify who can get connected to the national grid and how a fair billing system can be developed. In most countries, people who generate electricity from renew-

13. Godfrey Boyle (ed), *Renewable Energy: Power for a Sustainable Future*, Chapter 5, 'Hydroelectricity' Janet Ramage, Oxford University Press, Oxford, 2004, page 190.

able sources can sell into the grid when they have a surplus and buy from the grid when they are short. This has yet to happen in Ireland. Finally, if the government wishes to promote alternative energy it will have to develop systems where capital costs are subsidised.

## Bio-energy

The term bio-energy refers to energy which comes directly from living matter like wood, grass or animal waste, in contrast to energy from fossilised matter. It can be burned directly to provide heat and light or transformed into biofuels. Wood has been the dominant form of energy used by *homo sapiens* during the past one million years. It is still the most accessible form of energy used in many traditional societies. Though statistics are notoriously difficult to come by, it is estimated that bioenergy accounts for about one third of the primary energy consumption in economically poor countries.[14] When I began working with the T'boli people in hills of South Cotabato in the Philippines in 1980 bio-energy was the only energy source available to the people.

Since Neolithic times, wood has been used for cooking food and heating dwellings in Ireland. By the time of the Act of Union in 1800 the woodlands of Ireland had almost vanished. The wood had been used for shipbuilding and charcoal had been used for smelting. Woods accounted for around 1% of the total land area. Little changed in relation to planting trees until after Independence in 1921 when the government began a forestry programme. By the 1990 almost 8% of Ireland's land area was covered with trees – mainly non-native stika spruce. The amount of wood coverage in Ireland compares very unfavourably with other European countries where up to 25% of the land area is covered with forests. The sad part of it is that Ireland has one of the best climates in Europe for growing trees

---

14. Godfrey Boyle (ed), *Renewable Energy: Power For A Sustainable Future*, Chapter 4, 'Bioenergy' by Stephen Larkin, Janet Ramage and Johathan Scurlock, Oxford University Press, Oxford, 2004, page 108.

and we should be using this advantage to supply our energy needs. There is a lot of scope for short-rotation coppiced wood crops like willow which is suitable for turning into wood pellets for home heating systems.

Like fossil fuel, bio-energy is ultimately derived from the sun through photosynthesis. This is the process whereby plants take water and carbon dioxide from the environment and by using sunlight as energy convert these into starches, sugars and cellulose. In the process they release off oxygen. The energy which is stored can be used in multiple ways as food and energy for the human community. One of the great advantages of bio-energy is that it does not create more carbon dioxide and so can contribute to the battle against global warming.

Bio-energy is derived from two sources – energy crops and waste. One common form is to use fast growing trees like willow for wood chip heating. It is also possible to use straw left over from cereal production for heating but the main disadvantage is that straw bales are bulky. The world's largest straw-fired power station at Sutton near Ely in Cambridgeshire was opened in 2000. The plant is located near the cereal producing area of Britain which reduces transport costs. The output capacity is 36 megawatts and the cost of construction was £60 million.

One of the most important factors in the modern debate about bio-energy is yield. Unless there is a good yield from the crop, the economic argument for promoting modern bio-energy does not stack up.

Anaerobic digestion of animal waste matter is also a form of bio-energy. It involves the decomposition of animal waste by bacteria in the absence of air. This process releases biogas, especially methane, which can be used for heating or generating electricity. Since animal manure can be a significant source of greenhouse gases, this process contributes to lowering global warming as well as protecting streams, rivers and lakes from eutrophication. Anaerobic digestion is used in many countries in the majority world. China is particularly famous for this kind of energy. There was a major drive to promote the technology in China in the 1970s but many of the models later failed. A more

recent drive in the 1990s with better technology has brought this
technology to about 5 million families.[15]

Given the reality of peak-oil and spiraling oil prices, biofuels
are particular attractive in a country like Ireland which has no
indigenous oil and which uses 4 to 5 billion litres of fuel *per
annum* to fuel our cars and trucks. Brazil for example has a highly
successful gasohol programme. Gasohol is made by fermenting
sugar-cane which is high in sugars. The Brazilians began this
process soon after the first oil crisis in 1973. Even though gasoline prices became relatively cheap again in the 1980s and the
1990s, the Brazilians continued with their scheme and saved the
country $40 billion in foreign exchange. Most vehicles in the
country run on gasohol with a 26% ethanol content. Production
has reached 15 billion litres per annum and reduced greenhouse
gases in the process. If Ireland intends to go down this route, it
will need to make it economic for farmers to grow biofuels. It
will also have to invest in processing units and a national supply
system of filling stations which will make these fuels readily
available at competitives prices when compared to oil.

One major concern about bio-energy is that it will place new
pressures on land use. Some of the spin-offs can be very positive
like a revitalisation of rural life and an adequate return for the
farmer who is producing bio-crops. However, there might well
be a clash between using land to grow food for the local population and using land to grow energy crops for wealthy people living locally or in other parts of the world. Already the Biotech industry is using the oil shortage and global warming as a new
platform on which to promote their products. At BIO 2006, the
annual convention of the Biotechnology Industry Organisation
in Chicago in May 2006, there was a call for government support
to promote 'biofuels'. The 20,000 people who attended heard
speaker after speaker claim that biofuels can wean the US away
from what President Bush called their 'addiction to oil'. The industry is calling for serious funding to research how to create
ethanol fuels from biotech crops.

---

15. Ibid, 129.

But, of course, biofuels will not address the 'addiction' to oil. The Department of Energy in the US estimates the US biomass potential at about 160 million tonnes per year. This could substitute for 1 million barrels of oil daily. However, in 2006 the US consumed 21 million barrels each day. To grow crops to produce the equivalent of 21 million barrels of oil each day would need twice the arable land in the US, all growing genetically modified soy. So other strategies will be needed to address the addiction to oil. In reality, nothing is going to be found that will be a direct easy substitute for cheap and ready access to oil products which have been the dominant feature of human life in terms of settlement patterns and agriculture since World War II.[16]

Another concern is that some of the crops that are being sown as food crops, like oil seed rape, take a lot of nutrients from the soil. If it is cultivated in a monocrop fashion, it will build up crop specific pests and diseases in the soil. This is the reason why oil seed rape must be grown on a four year cycle to prevent the depletion of the nutrients in the soil. Even if the area of tillage was increased dramatically to 800,000 hectares and one quarter was devoted to oil seed rape, we would still have an energy crisis. The return from oil seed rape is estimated to be between 1,100 and 1,600 litres per hectare. The bottom line is that it would be wrong to fool ourselves into thinking that biofuel will solve our energy problem. It will not. Even with maximum cultivation, the fuels available from rape seed oil would only power between 6% and 7% of our national fleet.[17]

There cannot be an easy transfer from the versatility of fossil fuel to biomass energy for the simple reason that we would have to increase consumption of all primary production on land by 50%. This is patently impossible because even now we are 20% above what the planet can sustainable provide.[18]

16. Charles Shaw, 'Biotechnology Still Fuelling Controversy', www. gmwatch/org/23/05/2006, pages 1 to 5.
17. 'Pouring Cold Water on Biofuel Fantasy', *The Local Planet*, February-April 2006, pages 6 and 7.
18. Tim Flannery, *The Weather Makers*, op. cit., page 78.

*Solar Power*

Solar thermal devices are one of the best ways to use the sun's energy to produce hot water. They can be fitted on the south side of buildings to maximise exposure to the sun. These devices are reliable. Since they produce hot water they lower energy costs for the whole household. Even though there is great potential for solar thermal heating in Ireland we have been among the slowest in Europe to adopt this technology. In 2001, for example, Sweden, though situated further north than Ireland, installed 7 times more solar panels than we did in Ireland.

Solar energy using photovoltaic (PV) technology is another benign source of the sun's energy. It is generated when light hits the pure crystal of a semiconductor material like silicon. In the process electrons are prized loose from the atoms to which they are attached and produce an electric current. The efficiency rate of the conversion has increased dramatically in the past decade. It is now well over 30% efficient in converting the energy in sunlight into usable energy.[19] Unlike coal, oil or gas, no materials are consumed while generating the electricity. Furthermore it converts sunlight into electricity directly without having to go through an intermediate thermal phase. The technology is characterised by low energy density though efficiency rates have increased dramatically in recent years. Since it is a stand-alone system, it can occupy a few centimetres or a few kilometres. It is also very flexible, meeting small or larger needs. This ability to meet local needs is a very important characteristic from the democratic perspective. This form of energy frees people from being dependent on a large centralised grids whether these are controlled by the state agency, as in Ireland, or powerful energy corporations as in many other countries.

PV technology should have a major role in providing energy in counties like Britain and Ireland. It is particularly well suited to an urban environment because unlike wind energy you don't

19. David Fleming, 'Building a lean economy for a fuel-poor-future', in *Before the Wells Run Dry: Ireland's Transition to Renewable Energy*, Richard Douthwaite (ed), Lilliput Press, Dublin, 2003, page 103.

have to install a turbine on your roof and no other structures like cables are necessary to make it operative. Unfortunately, it is still quite expensive, partly because economies of scale have not driven down prices. For example, in 2004 the cost of fitting a house in Britain with PV technology was £20,000.[20] If, on the other hand, PV technology were integrated into new buildings it would make the technology much less expensive. The building industry or consumer will not make this choice unless there is serious support from the government for this well tried and flexible technology. This might come in two forms – changes to the building regulations to require solar technology in new buildings, and financial support whether this is delivered through direct support or tax breaks to make the technology less expensive. As the price of fossil fuel continues to rise, alternative energy becomes even more desirable in terms, not just of saving on energy and green house gas emissions, but also in financial terms.

It is important that PV systems should be able to be connected to the wider electric grid. For this to happened there needs to be a 'grid-commutated inventer'. This transforms DC power from the PV system into AC power at the voltage and frequency which is standard in the grid. To meet the electricity needs of an average house, if one excludes heating, one would need about nine square metres of panels. The roofs of many houses in Ireland could accommodate such panels.

Appropriately enough, St Oliver Plunket's Church in West Belfast became the first church in Ireland to install solar photovoltaic panels (PV) on its south facing roof. It is estimated that the installation will reduce the carbon dioxide emissions into the atmosphere by around 1600 kilograms each year. The solar energy system was funded both by the parish itself and the Energy Saving Trust of Northern Ireland Electricity's Smart programme. Something like this could be replicated all over the country.

Other countries have also promoted PV systems. During the past 10 years PV power has grown at between 30% and 40% per

---

20. Martin Hodgson, 'Solar eclipse', *The Guardian*, Environment supplement, 3 November 2004, page 12.

annum. The growth has been particularly significant in Germany, the US and Japan. Germany launched the 1000 Roof Programme in 1995. This installed about 2250 systems of about 6 megawatts in total.

Solar energy is also very important in Germany particularly since it has decided to phase out its nuclear energy power plants. A 1991 law forced energy companies to buy renewable power from operators at a generous price. An estimated 10,000 people are employed in this sector.

Japan and to a lesser extent the US have led the way in PV technology. Public disenchantment with nuclear spurred a major growth in solar energy in Japan. By the early 1990s the Japanese government began offering generous subsidies for installing solar panels in households. As a result electricity from solar power is now cheaper than electricity from the nuclear grid. Japan now produces more solar power than any other country.

The US has begun a 1 million solar roof initiative. In May 2006, two start-up companies, New Solar Ventures and Solar Torx, with the help of venture capital, negotiated with the state of New Mexico to build what will probably be the world's largest solar power venture on 3,200 acres of mostly public land near the Mexican border. The proposed facility will be 60 times larger than the present world leader which is in Bavaria in Germany. The state government has helped by providing a sweetheart deal in terms of leasing 640 state-owned acres close to the town of Deming. The company spokesperson, state officials and environmentalists are optimistic that the plant will generate 300 megawatts of energy. This would be considered enough to provide power for 240,000 homes within a period of five years. They also plan to build a factory to make 10 foot by 5 foot solar panels.[21] The Belgian government has introduced a

---

21. Rody Scheer, 'World's Largest Solar Farm Taking Root in New Mexico Desert', May 2, 2006, www.emagazine.com/view/?3192 04/05/2006. page 1 of 1.

50% investment subsidy for grid-connnected, building-integrated PV installations up to 3 kwp.[22]

The price of installing a PV system is continuing to fall as a result of improved technology, competition and the greater capacity of suppliers to service the growing market. Improvement in electronic engineering will also mean thinner wafers which will increase efficiency. Furthermore, the running costs of PV systems is very low.

But the potential for this form of power seems to be much greater. The environmental organisation Greenpeace and the European PV Industry Association published a report in 2001 entitled *Solar Generation: Solar Electricity for over 1 Billion People and 2 Million Jobs by 2020*. The document envisages 200 gigawatts of installed PV capacity worldwide, supplying 1 billion off-grid and 82 million grid-connected users. Over 30 million of those would be in Europe. By 2020 some 60% of PV production would be located in Asia, Africa or Latin America. This would create over 2 million fulltime jobs. By 2040 the report believes that PV systems could be generating 9000 terowatt-hours and thereby meet one quarter of the global electricity needs.[23]

A 2006 report on energy by the charity Christian Aid sees small-scale solar power as the best option for many millions of small communities who at present lack electricity. They estimate that it would cost about $50 billion to provide the 500 million people living in sub-Saharan Africa with renewable energy.[24] There are huge possibilities for growth in PV power especially in rural communities in Latin America, Africa and South East Asia.

The churches should also be supporting every effort to improve energy efficiency. Christian Ecology Link have published a paper entitled *Faith and Power: The Case for a Low Consumption,*

---

22. *The Future for Renewable Energy*, EUREC Agency, 2002, James & James (Science Publishers) ltd, 35-37 William Road, London, NW 1 3ER, page 33.
23. Godfrey Boyle, op.cit., page 100.
24. John Vidal, 'Africa climate change could kill millions', *The Guardian*, 13 May 2006, page 25.

*Non-Nuclear, Energy Strategy.*[25] The document points out that
only 3.6% of electricity in Britain comes from renewable sources.
Groups like The Energy Saving Trust advise clients how to best
save energy.

## Tidal Energy

The movement of tides is a result of the gravitational pull of the
moon, and to a lesser extent of the sun, on the oceans. They happen twice a day. Energy generated from the movement of the
tides was used in both England and France in the Middle Ages
to grind corn. There is a relatively small tidal generating station
at the Rance Estuary in France. It generates 240 megawatts and
has operated successfully since the mid 1960s. In some areas,
tides are funnelled through estuaries, which can increase their
speed considerably as happens in the Severn Estuary in Britain.
One of the principle ways of trapping tidal energy is through the
use of tidal barrages. They are placed in a suitable location in an
estuary and are engineered in such a way as to extract the maximum amount of energy from the rise and fall of the tide and use
that to drive turbines that will generate electricity. It is necessary
to have a mean range of at least 5 metres in order for it to be viable and to compete economically with other renewable sources
of energy.[26] According to Professor John Ringwood, dean of engineering at NUI Maynooth, selected locations along the east
coast of Ireland, especially off the Antrim coast, offer the best
possibilities for tidal energy.

Wave energy is generated by wind as it blows across the
ocean. Scientists are now aware that waves created by a storm in
the mid-Atlantic will travel all the way to the coast of Ireland or
Scotland. All the energy in wave energy is concentrated in the
top 50 metres of the ocean. The goal of wave energy technologies

25. Christian Ecology Link, March 2006, *Faith and Power: The Case for a
Low Consumption, Non-Nuclear, Energy Strategy*, 3 Bond Street, Lancaster,
LAI 3ER. www.christian-ecology.org.uk
26. Les Duckers, 'Wave Energy' in Godfrey Boyle (ed), *Renewable
Energy*, Oxford University Press, pp 204-240.

is to capture this highly concentrated source of energy and to make it available as electricity.

The European Marine Energy Centre (EMEC) is situated off the coast of Strommness in the Orkney Islands. It is in the forefront of the pioneering research and development on wave and tidal energy. The Centre is designed to help those who are actively researching and designing products to produce wave energy with a purpose-built testing facility. At the moment EMEC operates four test berths at its wave energy site. Each of these are located about 2 kilometres from the shore in about 50 metres of water. Sensitive instruments at the substation at Billia Croo measure the output from different wave energy converters.

The main developer at the moment is Ocean Power Delivery (OPD). This company has been testing its wave energy converter called Pelamis since the summer of 2004. Pelamis has a similar output to a modern wind turbine. The 750 kilowatt prototype is 120 metres long and contains three Power Conversion Modules, each rated at 259 kilowatts. In the summer of 2005 the device was still being tested. With the knowledge gained thus far, the developers are hoping that a typical 30 megawatt station would occupy a square kilometre of ocean and produce electricity for 20,000 homes. Twenty of these wave farms could provide sufficient power for a city like Edinburgh which has a population of 453,000 people. One of the main problems with wave energy is the regular gales and storms on the North Atlantic. The equipment would have to be both secure and robust to counteract this.

The Forum for Renewable Energy Development Scotland is confident that there could be one large marine power station, generating 1300 megawatts of electricity by the year 2020. The complex would be made up of a series of 10 to 20 megawatt units positioned along the coast. EMEC believes that if this technology is properly developed there could 'massive potential' for green energy in Scotland.[27]

Ireland, especially the Atlantic coast, should also be an ideal location for wave energy. In 2006, tidal and tidal current energy

27 'Making waves in renewable energy', *SEPAVIEW: The magazine of the*

is in its infancy. Ireland took a significant step in developing wave energy with the opening of a wave test site off the coast of Spiddal in County Galway in March 2006. A joint operation between the Marine Institute and Sustainable Energy Ireland (SEI) will open up a 37 hectare site for engineers, designers and entrepreneurs to test their models.

Already one technology called Wavebob, developed by William Dick, is being tested in the area. The top of the Wavebob rests just below the surface of the water and bobs up and down to the rhythm of the waves. This motion drives hydraulic pistons, which in turn push oil through a motor that drives a generator which in turn produces electricity. The technology manager of the Marine Institute, Eoin Sweeny is convinced that since wave technology is in its infancy, Ireland could become a world leader in this form of renewable energy. He believes that once we crack the technology we could export it and create about 2,000 jobs here at home. William Dick believes that there is huge potential for wave power and that it could meet the needs of the Irish grid.[28] Even by 2010 he would like to see two or three wave farms off the west coast of Ireland, off Donegal, Mayo and Clare.

It will need careful nurturing by national and local government so that the necessary finance is available for research and development costs and initial capital investment. Professor Ringwood believes that 'Ireland has the best wave climate in the world. There is no better place to tap into this resource.'[29]

He is convinced that if Ireland invests in wave and tidal energy it could become a world leader in this technology in the same way that Denmark is the world leader today in wind energy because of decisions that were taken by the Danish government thirty years ago.[30] If the resources are invested now, Ireland

_Scottish Environment Protection Agency_, July / August 2005, issue 25, pages 16 -17.

28. 'Trying to fathom wave power', _Irish Independent_, Special Report, 29 March 2006. page 14.

29. Dick Ahlstrom, 'The new wave; harnessing the sea', _The Irish Times_, 17 July 2006, page 6.

30. Dick Ahlstrom, ibid.

could become an exporter of ocean technology to other parts of the world.

In Britain, the Royal Commission on Environmental Pollution (RCEP) complained that wave power and undersea turbines have received little government support despite their huge potential. The following skewed public expenditure announcement on energy saw a mere £42 million for tidal and wave energy, £1 million for solar, £30 million for small-scale renewable energy initiatives and a huge £2,200 million for the Nuclear Decommissioning Authority.[31]

*Wind Energy*

Wind energy has been used by communities for a long time, usually to grind cereals, pump water or perform other mechanical tasks. Before electricity was widely available from a central grid, wind turbines were used to generate electricity. In the late 1940s my neighbours in Nenagh had such a system for generating power. With the introduction of the rural electrification system in the early 1950s, wind turbines almost disappeared. Since the mid-1980s they have begun to reappear, this time driven by the knowledge that fossil fuels are running out and that wind turbines do not emit carbon dioxide. As the number of wind turbines both on land and at sea began to increase, the cost of wind energy began to fall considerably. The energy produced by wind turbines depends on the speed of the wind and the technology used to construct the wind turbine. Developments in the area of aerodynamics have also increased the efficiency of wind turbines in recent years. David Fleming writes that a typical wind turbine in the year 2000 had an output of about 225 kilowatts, producing a theoretical 2 million kilowatt-hours (kwh) each year. This would provide sufficient energy, excluding transport, for thirty households where energy efficiency was not

31. *Faith and Power: The Case for A Low Consumption, Non-Nuclear, Energy,* page 3 Strategy, Christian Ecology Link, 3 Bond Street, Lancaster FAI 3ER, see www.christian-ecology.org.uk

a priority. The households would double to sixty if they were well insulated.[32]

Opponents of wind energy often reject the technology because of the noise factor but the more modern turbines are much quieter than their predecessors. There are also complaints that wind farms impact negatively on the landscape. While wind farms should not be placed in particularly picturesque places or in the path ways of migrating birds, the fact that they do not emit greenhouse gases is a huge plus for the industry from an environmental perspective.

Given the fact that we are situated in Western Europe on the Atlantic coast and that most weather systems come off the ocean, Ireland is uniquely positioned to benefit from wind energy. Denmark began developing wind energy in the 1980s. Currently, 20% of it energy comes from the wind. Unlike Denmark, Ireland was slow to develop wind energy. In Denmark much of the wind energy is owned by small co-operatives. A community buys a turbine and uses the electricity which it generates for its own purposes. More than 30% of windmills in Denmark are owned by community groups. One would hope that community groups in Ireland might opt for similar schemes.

Wind power has great potential here in Ireland. Only a miniscule part of that potential has been actualised to date.[33] In 2005, more than 300 megawatts of wind farms received offers to connect to the national grid. This is in addition to the 500 megawatts already generated by 50 wind farms in different parts of the country from Kerry to Wexford, Tipperary, Monaghan and Donegal. The largest wind-farm in Ireland, off the coast of Wicklow, is operated by a company called Airtricity. This company was set up in 1998 and by 2006 it was worth over €800 million. The founder of Airtricity, Eddie O'Connor is convinced that there is not sufficient support for alternative energy

32. David Fleming, 'Building a lean economy for a fuel poor future', in *Before the Wells Run Dry*, op.cit., page 103.
33. 'Wind Energy' by Derek Taylor in Godfrey Boyle, (ed), *Renewable Energy*, Oxford University Press, pp. 242-296.

in Ireland. It would take just 1,000 off-shore turbines to power all the households in Ireland. O'Connor believes that much more needs to be done in Ireland given the fact that Ireland imports over 90% of its energy from abroad. This is significantly more than the EU average which stands at just over 50%.

By 2006, the wind lobby in Ireland believes that Ireland can reach the EU target of generating 13.3% of its electricity from renewable sources by 2010. Tom Cowhig, who is chairman of the Irish Wind Energy Association, feels that we must promote renewable energy sources if we are to avoid an energy crisis.[34] It is interesting that in 2004 wind over took hydo as the dominant renewable energy source in Ireland, according to research conducted by Sustainable Energy Ireland.[35]

The first large scale urban wind turbine in Ireland was built at Dundalk Institute of Technology (DKIT). The turbine cost €1.1 million to install and it will save DKIT around €150,000 and therefore pay for itself in 8 or 9 years. The DKIT turbine is the world's first large turbine on a college campus. It will cut the electricity bill for DKIT in half. As a contribution to global warming it will cut carbon dioxide emissions by 1,100 tonnes annually.[36]

Wind power would receive a major boost if there was an interconnector between Ireland and Britain. It would allows us to export electricity when there is a surplus and import energy where there is a shortage because the wind is not blowing.

A group of researchers from a small engineering company in Britain have teamed up with aerospace designers to develop a new design for wind energy turbines which does two things. It overcomes some of the antipathy towards wind energy. This new turbine, which is about five metres long, is designed in a triple helix form on a vertical axis which makes it almost noise

34. Frank McDonald, 'Power Struggle', *The Irish Times*, Weekend Review, 14 January 2006, page 2
35. *Energy in Ireland 1990-2004*, op. cit., page 2.
36. 'Wind energy goes urban', *The Irish Independent*, Special Report, 20 March 2006, page 15.

free. Secondly, wind farms until now were normally situated on hills or exposed areas in the countryside, often far away from towns and cities. This triple helix form on a vertical axis will, in fact, perform more efficiently in cities where wind directions may vary minute by minute. The designers claim that the turbine can produce around 10,000 kilowwatt hours a year on an average wind speed of 5.8 metres per second. They also claim that it could provide sufficient electricity for five energy-efficient homes. The installation cost for a 6 kilowatt turbine will be around £28,000.[37] This new wind technique could have huge potential to deliver energy directly to where it is consumed without routing it through a long grid where a significant percentage of the energy is lost.

## Hydrogen

A word of caution is necessary when one begins to talk about a hydrogen economy. Many people talk in what might be described as an evolutionary energy perspective. Prior to the 19th century, energy was predominantly wood and human and animal power. The 19th century was dominated by coal. Oil took the front seat in the 20th century. It seems that natural gas will be in poll position for the beginning of the 21st century, but all eyes are on developing a hydrogen economy. At the core of a proposed hydrogen economy is the hydrogen fuel cell. This is not a new technology. Hydrogen fuel cells were invented by Sir William Robert Grove in the 19th century but were not used much until the space agency in the US, NASSA, developed them for their Apollo and Gemini space programme. Fuel cells are devices with parts that move; they take in hydrogen and oxygen and give off water and electricity. These cells could be used in a stationary position to develop electricity, and as fuel cells for transport. The cells are stackable flat plates. Each cell produces one volt. So the power output is determined by the size of the stack of cells.

---

37. John Vidal, 'Radical turbine aims to take wind power to cities', *The Guardian*, 2 June 2006, page 4.

Iceland is the world's most energy efficient country. 70% of its energy is produced from local renewable sources, mainly hydro and geothermal. Imported fossil fuel is used in the transport sector but Icelanders are determined to substitute fossil fuel with hydrogen within a few years. It plans to produce hydrogen by using its abundant geothermal energy. In 2003, it opened the first hydrogen filling station in the capital, Reykjavik. Many of the major car manufactures are trying to develop hydrogen power cars. In 2002, Toyota produced it FCHV fuel-cell car. Competitors in Japan and the US are investing a lot of money in developing their own hydrogen cars.

A major problem at the moment is that the technology is expensive, but economies of scale could bring down the price of these devices. There are still major problems in producing hydrogen and distributing it to depots. Where are the 200 million cars presently in the US fleet going to be manufactured? Are we going to be able to substitute hydrogen filling stations for gasoline ones without any disruption? I do not think so. Still Jeremy Rifkins in his book *The Hydrogen Economy* promotes hydrogen as a way of decentralising energy distribution. He believes that people should not be dependent on centralised grids

*Sweden*

Sweden has taken a bold step by planning to wean itself off oil by the year 2020. This obviously is a major undertaking and it has involved the co-operation of people from various walks of life. The planning committee is composed of car makers, scientists, farmers, industrialists, civil servants, environmentalists and politicians, including the prime minister, and people from environmental groups. The Minister in charge of sustainable development has promised 'that our dependency on oil should be broken by 2020 and there shall always be better alternatives to oil, which means no house should need oil for heating, and no driver should need to turn solely to gasoline'.[38]

38. John Vidal, 'Sweden plans to be world's first oil-free economy', *The Guardian*, 8 February 2006. www.guardian.co.uk/print/),,5394081-110970,00.html 08/02/2006.

A government spokesperson gave the following reasons for planning this extraordinary change in energy use. He said, 'a Sweden free of fossil fuel would give us enormous advantages, not least by reducing the impact from fluctuations in oil prices … We want to be both mentally and technically prepared for a world without oil. The plan is a response to global climate change, rising petroleum prices and warnings by some experts that the world may soon be running out of oil.'[39]

Sweden's energy profile is interesting. Most of the electricity needs are generated by hydro power and nuclear energy. Fossil fuels account for 32% of Sweden's energy needs. Most of this drives the transport sector.[40] Unlike it neighbour Norway, Sweden has no gas or petroleum reserves so fazing out dependency on oil makes a lot of sense. Whether it can be achieved by 2020 is another question, but at least there is a debate going on in the country, actions are being taken and there is widespread support among the public for this creative initiative. Sweden is ahead of its EU partners in that 26% of energy consumed comes from renewable sources, whereas the average in the rest of the EU is 6%. This has been achieved by grants and green taxes.

*Ireland*

The contrast between the integrated response in Sweden and Ireland could not be greater. Ireland is the 9th most oil-dependent economy in the world. While the average EU reliance on oil for energy needs is 43% Ireland is in a very vulnerable position since 64% of our energy needs are provided by oil.[41] This reliance on oil has increase dramatically since the arrival of what is called the Celtic Tiger in the mid-1990s. This led to a huge increase in motorcars and also in the demands for energy which was fuelled by the building boom. An EU report entitled *Transport and Environment: Facing a Dilemma 2005* shows that

39. ibid, page 1.
40. Gwladys Fouche, 'Split decisions', *The Guardian, Society/Guardian/ Environment*, 14 June 2006, page 9.
41. Frank McDonald, 'Power Struggle', *The Irish Times*, Weekend Reivew, 14 January 2006, page 2.

emissions from cars, buses and freight transport has increased
by a massive 130% in Ireland between 1990 and 2003. This compares unfavourably with an average increase in emissions of
23% from the transport section in 32 European countries sur-
veyed over the same period.[42]

Out of a budget of over €50 billion the Minister for
Communications, Marine and Natural Resources, had the paltry
sum of €65 million earmarked to be spent over five years for
conversion of homes, transport systems and businesses to renewable energy. On 27 March 2006, the minister announced the
'Greener Home' scheme. €25 million have been allocated to
cover all aspects of the scheme from wood pellets, to geothermal
and solar. The sum allotted will only cover between 5,000 and
7,000 homes which is little enough when considers what needs
to be done. An individual home owner can get a grant of €4,200
for installing a wood chip burner or pellet boiler, €6,500 for geothermal energy pumps and €300 per square metre for solar
panels up to 12 square metres.[43] The Minister said that these initiatives are expected to save up to 54,000 barrels of oil per
annum and 23,000 tonnes of carbon dioxide. While the scheme is
to be welcomed, it is only a beginning. The minister must recognise that retrofitting existing houses – which in most cases is what
will happen – is much more expensive than installing renewable
energy systems when they are being built. The minister ought to
look at Denmark, Germany and Sweden who have a well developed alternative energy sector. The German government offers
long-term, low interest loans and income-tax credits to offset the
major costs of setting up alternative energy sources, whether it is
from photovoltaic or wind. The government also helps companies
who are meeting this growing demand for alternative energy. In
2003, they were more than 300 companies supplying solar panels
in Germany. There were more than 2,000 wind installations

---

42. Jamie Smyth, 'Ireland's greenhouse gases show fastest rise', *The Irish
Times*, 28 March 2006, page 1.
43. Mark Brennock, 'Renewable energy grants for households', *The Irish
Times*, 27 March 2006, page 5.

feeding into the grid. In Germany producers of alternative energy get premium prices when they feed into the national grid.

It seems that the minister and the rest of the Irish government have failed to realise that what has been allotted for developing renewable sources of energy is just a drop in the ocean in terms of what is needed. Given that we are fast approaching the end of the fossil fuel era, and that a potential catastrophe is lurking with global warming, there ought to be an integrated 'war-like' effort, initiated by government, to wean the Irish economy off its dependence on oil, coal and gas.

Hopefully the publication of Forfás, *A baseline Assessment of Ireland's Oil Dependency: Key Policy Considerations* in April 2006, which showed that Ireland ranked third highest among the EU 25 member states in terms of *per capita* oil consumption in 2002, will focus minds in the government to take this challenge seriously. The report also predicted that the supply of cheap oil will peak during the next 10 to 15 years and that this will pose major problems for the global economy. It recommends that Ireland develop a national strategy to deal with this eventuality.

One positive development during the past few years was the establishment of Sustainable Energy Ireland (SEI). The organisation was established under the aegis of the Sustainable Energy Act 2002, in May of that year. Its mission is to promote and assist in the development of sustainable energy. This is meant to cover a number of areas in the energy field like the production of sustainable energy at economically profitable prices and the supply of that energy to customers. Its remit relates mainly to improving energy efficiency, developing renewable energy sources and reducing the impact of energy production, especially in respect to greenhouse gas emissions. It is also tasked with raising awareness about renewable energy by supplying the public with advice on best practice.[44] It has published pamphlets on sustainable energy and energy efficiency.

---

44. *Energy in Ireland 1990-2004, Trends, issues, forecasts and indicators*, SEI Sustainable Energy Ireland, Energy Policy Statistical Support Unit, January 2006, page 1.

CHAPTER EIGHT

# Peak Oil and Transport

*Peak-Oil*

'Peak-oil' does not mean that oil will run out tomorrow. What it does mean is that 60% of the oil which is in the ground has already been used. Oil extraction follows a bell-curve pattern. Initially extraction costs are minimal and the oil that is made available is the lighter crude. For example, in the 1940s the return for 1 barrel invested in drilling for oil was 100 barrels of oil. After a certain period of time it becomes more expensive to extract the oil. Companies have to pump water or carbon-dioxide into the well to facilitate the extraction. By 2004, every barrel used to extract oil only produced 10 barrels of oil and the number is falling as the amount of oil available from a well decreases and becomes more difficult to access. In 1999, when the UK's oil fields in the North Sea peaked, they were pumping 3 million barrels of oil each day. By the end of 2005 they were down to two barrels each day. The Irish Academy of Engineering have estimated that for every barrel of oil currently being added to certified reserves, five are being consumed. So with demand outstripping supply prices will continue to rise.[1]

A similar pattern is emerging in other major oil producing nations – Indonesia, Norway and Venezuela. Even the oil companies are beginning to admit that the day of cheap oil is over. Chevron, the second largest oil company in the US took out double page advertisements in some of the world's leading business newspapers like *The Financial Times* and *The Economist*. The ad stated that, 'energy will be one of the defining issues of this cent-

---

1. Frank McDonald, 'When the Well Runs Dry', *The Irish Times, Weekend Review*, 15 July 2006, page 1.

ury. One thing is clear, the era of easy oil is over … Many of the world's oil and gas fields are maturing. And new energy discoveries are mainly occurring in places where resources are difficult to extract – physically, technically, economically and politically.' The advertisement was signed by David O'Reilly, chairman of the corporation.[2] That should be a clear warning that the days of cheap oil and all that it spawned are over.

'Peak-Oil' happened in the US oil industry in the early 1970s, the time when, ironically, the US had reached a peak in oil production. Because the industry is often at full throttle when peak-oil happens, people often do not notice it immediately. It may only be a decade later when both production costs are rising and extraction rates are declining that people realise that peak-oil happened and the reserves in the new discoveries are less than what is consumed.

When is peak-oil going to happen on a global scale? It is not easy to say for a number of reasons. The bulk of oil now is coming from the Middle East and Asia, two areas of the world which are notoriously unstable politically. So accessing oil in these regions may become both more difficult, more dangerous and more costly. In addition, many commentators on peak-oil question the accuracy of the oil reserves which many countries claim they have. They point to the fact that many of the oil-exporting countries in the Middle East doubled their reserves over night in the 1980s when it appeared that OPEC might impose a rationing system on production. Since production ceilings would be based on known reserves, it was in the interest of many of these countries who have nothing else to export except oil to 'cook the books' and expand their reserves.

Matthew Simmons, chairman of the Wall Street energy investment company Simmons, told a conference in Edinburgh in April 2005 that 'there is a big chance that Saudi Arabia actually peaked production in 1981. We have no reliable data. Our data collection system for oil is rubbish. I suspect that if we had we would find that we are over-producing in most of our major fields and that we should be throttling back. We may have past the point.'[3] He went on to say that demand was pulling away from supply and that it could be catastrophic if we do not anticipate when peak oil comes.[4]

Finally the arrival of global peak-oil is been speeded up by the energy needs of countries whose economies are expanding like India, Brazil and China. The demand for oil in China has doubled over the past ten years. It is now the second largest oil consumer after the United States. Given the needs of its people and the developing economy, China expects to double its need for oil in the next fifteen years which would speed up the arrival of an oil crisis. Some experts predict that oil could be over $100 a barrel by 2010. With less supply and a 2% growth in demand, it seems logical that nations will bid against each other to secure supplies and this will drive prices even higher.

The oil industry is attempting to counter some of the arguments put forward by the proponents of peak oil. In June 2005, Lord Browne, the chief executive of BP, told the German magazine *Der Spiegel* that in the medium term the price of oil will drop back to around $40 a barrel. In the long run even $20 or $30 is possible. In support of this claim he pointed out that large oilfields are still being found in West Africa. He also believes that Canadian oil sand can now be exploited profitably.[5]

The columnist George Monbiot was particularly incensed by both Shell and BP which have been attempting to rebrand their companies as environmentally friendly. They have published numerous advertisements on TV and in newspapers highlighting their Green credentials in the search for alternative, non-carbon energy sources in the area of solar panels and hydrogen fuel cells. Yet, in the above paragraph, Lord Browne is trying to settle nervous markets by claiming that oil prices would fall and the

---

3. John Vidal, 'Analyst fears global oil crisis in three years', *The Guardian* Society/Supplement, 26 April 2005. www.society.guardian.co.uk/print26/04/2005 page 1 of 2.
4. ibid.
5. Terry MacAlister, 'Oil price likely to fall, says Browne', *The Guardian*, 13 June 2006, page 23.

situation would return to normal. Browne knows this is a fallacy but as Monbiot wrote 'both companies are cleverer than they used to be. They have stopped pretending that climate change does not exist or that no one ever gets hurt by their projects. Shell even published a list of its recent legal convictions. But that doesn't mean they have stopped spinning.'[6]

Peak-oil proponents feel that transport, and especially suburban living will be the first casualty of peak-oil and the end of the oil era. In fact, agriculture, food production and distribution will be the areas of life most affected. Modern agriculture depends for its success on inorganic nitrogen and a host of herbicides, fungicides and insecticides, all of which are derived from oil. The connection is so extensive that Richard Manning could write an article in *Harper's Magazine*, entitled, 'The Oil we Eat'. Then there are the food processing and packaging industries which produce convenience foods. Manning writes that 'All together the food-processing industry in the United States uses about ten calories of fossil-fuel energy for every calorie of food energy it produces.'[7]

Manning goes on to make the point that this figure does not include the cost of transporting this food to depots and retail outlets all over the US, and now every country, and the fossil fuel which those living in suburbia use to buy their food in supermarkets and shopping malls. At the moment it costs 127 calories of fuel for every calorie of lettuce to fly a head of lettuce from the US to London.

Peak-oil and the consequent ending of the gasoline era will bring all this to an end. It will begin to unravel because there is simply no combination of alternative fuels which will allow us to live in such a wasteful way in the post peak-oil world. According to some commentators, one third of the large trucks on motorways in the US are carrying processed food. The cost of

6. George Monbiot, 'Behind the spin, the oil giants are more dangerous than ever', *The Guardian*, 13 June 2006, page 27.
7. Richard Manning, 'The Oil We Eat: Following the Food Chain Back to Iraq', *Harper's Magazine*, February 2004, page 44.

moving huge stocks of goods around in massive lorries will become very expensive. This will have two consequences: there will be a movement back to shopping locally and to buying our food directly from farmers' markets and, secondly, freight will be transferred back to the railways were it is less costly. Because of the massive increase in oil prices the food distribution network will begin to shift from an international focus to a local one. Many more people will become involved in food production, often driven by necessity. The present situation where only 2% of the population in the US are engaged in food production will be dramatically reversed.

The gradual disintegration of these huge distribution networks will free up space on our roads and point to the folly of investing such a huge amount of money in them in the first place. One way or another the days of continuous urban sprawl are limited as oil becomes less available and more expensive. David Williams, a columnist with *The Irish Independent*, is one of the few journalist who is raising these questions in Ireland in 2006. His column on 26 March 2006, entitled 'Be warned: the end of cheap oil will kill suburban dreams', addresses these issues.

One response to the suburban sprawl is the movement called the new urbanism. This sets out to promote diverse, compact and vibrant mixed-use communities. The most important contact points like shop, schools, churches and park could be reached within a ten minute walk from one's home or work place. These are the kinds of initiatives that public authorities in Ireland should be promoting, rather than pouring billions of euro into creating a way of living that literally has no future. We are going to have to live much more locally and provide many of the services we need, including food production, locally in the post peak-oil world.

It is worth pointing out that the collapse of the USSR in the late 1980s had a huge impact on Cuba since cheap oil from the Soviet Union was no longer available. Cuban agriculture used more agri-chemicals than their US counterparts. The abrupt ending of cheap oil led to a major drop in Gross Domestic

Product (GDP) but, more seriously, food began to run out and people began to experience hunger and malnutrition. The Cuban government encouraged organic farming in a variety of locations. Large scale government farms were broken up and distributed to a number of families who formed an agricultural cooperative. Urban gardens were encouraged even in parking lots and unused public land. Thousands of roof top gardens appeared. Small animals like chickens and rabbits were also raised on roof-tops. Since little petrochemicals were available, government scientists developed biological ways of controlling pests and increasing soil fertility. By the year 2000, the country had avoided a food crisis because food production was back to 90% of what it had been before their oil crisis and Cuban farmers were using one-twentieth of the energy which the US counterparts were using.[8]

Unfortunately, the unraveling of the oil-based living patterns could be very painful indeed. At present, most institutions – economic, political, and religious – are in denial, so where can we look to for leadership during this transition which could be violent and destructive?

*The future of the car*

Individuals, local communities and governments are going to have to tackle the fact that most of us are addicted to our own individual car. Given inward migration and continual economic growth, some commentators are talking about doubling the number of cars on the road in the next ten years. The prospect of this happening should send a shiver down the spine of every commuter. Rather than constantly building new motorways that become clogged with traffic within a few years of their completion, like the M50 Motorway around Dublin, we need to wean ourselves off cars.

The motorcar, and what it has made possible in terms of patterns of human living, was one of the most dominant influences

8. Dan Box, Tully Wakeman and Jeremy Smith, 'The End of Cheap Oil: The Consequences', *The Ecologist*, October 2005, pages 46 to 52.

on people and the planet in the 20th century. Until the dawn of the 20th century the majority of the human population lived in the countryside or in small rural towns. Those who lived in cities were able to access their work place, their shops and other amenities by walking or riding a street car. Though the motorcar did become available to a sizeable number of people in the US in the 1920s, the growth in the number of the cars was temporarily halted by the great depression in the 1930s and World War II in the early 1940s. After the war things began to change dramatically. Car numbers increased again and this new mobility made it possible for people who were living in unsatisfactory conditions in cities to move out into what actually became suburbs.

Economic activity in the US in the 1950s was dominated by two colossal and inter-related activities. There was a housing boom; most of the houses were built on land in the countryside close to the major cities. People were encouraged to get away from the cities and avoid both the smog from the smokestack industries and the general grittiness of post-war cities. Housing estates in suburbia were marketed as living in the idyllic countryside, away from the city with all its negative connotations. Each house had its lawn, but people interacted less and less with their neighbours.

As demand for houses in the suburbs continued, these estates were built further and further from the cities. Since there were few amenities in the suburbs, planners had to build a gigantic network of roads to connect people with their workplace, their shopping centre, their schools and other support systems which are essential for human well-being. The density pattern of these new suburbs was often too low to warrant public transport systems like rail networks or buses, so the automobile was the machine that made living in suburbs possible. Even before both partners in a marriage began to work outside the home, in the late 1960s, each suburban household needed two cars to function properly. The husband needed his car to get to work in the city and the wife needed a car for shopping, delivering children to their schools or other activities.

This urban sprawl expanded in the US and was eventually exported to Europe, Latin America and also to Asia during the latter part of the 20th century. One after another, countries experienced suburban housing booms followed by massive road building programmes which ate into the fertile farm land which surrounded many cities in the world. Construction companies, petrochemical industries and large scale retailers like Wal-Mart made fabulous profits from creating and servicing the suburbs so, naturally, politicians, planners, engineers and regulatory agencies facilitated the development in every possible way. Everything was done to create the illusion that this was the only viable way to live. Yet this now-preferred way of living was more and more in discontinuity with human settlement patterns of the past. People literally do not know their next door neighbours or feel any need to get to know them. There is very little sense of community. People seldom walk or cycle around the neighbourhood as almost every journey is made by car. As a consequence, people today are much more obese, less healthy and suffer from diseases like diabetes.

Ireland was one of the last countries in Western Europe to follow this pattern of human settlement. The house-building boom began in earnest the mid-1990s and has been followed by the construction of motorways fanning out from Dublin. Since the mid-1990s many people drive forty or fifty miles to work each day. People are spending more and more time sitting in their cars frustrated that they cannot move from A to B quickly. They are led to believe by planners and politicians that the solution to their problem is another motorway. Anyone who raises a question about this strategy is ignored, talked down or dismissed as stupid. The cost of the motorways has escalated. According to figures from the National Roads Authority (NRA) and the Auditor General, the original estimate for the National Development Plan which was to run from the year 2000 to 2006 was €5.6 billion. By 2002, the figure had jumped to $15 billion and in 2006 it emerged that the total amount of money spent on road construction since 1997 was €20 billion. This is a three-fold increase in cost for a product that might not be used for very long if predictions about the cost of oil bite sooner rather than later.[9]

At least the US, Britain, Germany and France got 60 or 70 years use of their motorways. We will be lucky if we get a decade and a half use for these roads. It would have been much wiser if the Irish government had taken seriously the fact that we are rapidly reaching the end of the oil era, and if we had invested our money in building houses in places where they can be serviced by public transport. This would have allowed us to invest the bulk of the €20 billion in forms of transport that would still be sustainable in a post peak-oil world.

Suburban living and commuting was made possible by the simple fact that oil was readily available and cheap since World War II. There was a shot across our bow in 1973 when the Organisation of Petroleum Exporting Countries (OPEC) imposed sanctions on the Minority World in retaliation for the US support for Israel in the Yom Kippur war. Oil prices increased dramatically and caused a recession right around the world. The impact of the Iran-Iraq war caused oil prices to rise again in the period 1979 to 1981. These crises should have acted as a wake up call, a reminder of the fact that the next oil crisis would be the final one, since we are dealing with a finite reality. Unfortunately, by the 1990s the old order had been restored and it appeared that we could continue to promote suburban living globally, and economic growth would continually indefinitely. In 1998, oil prices dipped to $10 a barrel and many people, even economists, were saying that it would continue at this price for the foreseeable future. That did not happen. In May 2006, it reached $75 a barrel and it will never be cheap again for the simple reason that we are reaching, or are about to reach 'peak-oil'.

What are the positive responses to peak-oil? In Germany the university city of Freiburg invested the equivalent of £6 per person on the provision of cycle lane and depots. All the main roads

---

9. Daniel McConnell, '€20bn roads bill a huge drain on the taxpayer', *The Sunday Independent*, 28 May 2006, page 12.

have cycle lanes and many continue right out into the country. Car usage fell and the number of trips made by bicycle jumped from 15% to 26%.[10]

In March 2006 in Britain, on the M606 and M62 special lanes were set aside for vehicles with multiple occupancy. This is another initiative to promote car sharing and free up the roads. Unfortunately, Ireland seems to be immune to these simple solutions. The redevelopment of O'Connell's Street in Dublin does not have provisions for a cycle lane. In fact we have been eroding our car fuel efficiency since 2002 with the trend towards buying larger cars and sports utility vehicles (SUVs). A report by consultants Byrne Ó Cléirigh pointed out that, while internationally there has been swing towards more fuel efficient cars, Ireland's record is 'virtually static' or even getting worse with the advent of larger cars. The report, which was presented to the government, has claimed that greenhouse gas emissions for Ireland has to be revised upwards by 300,000 tonnes because many people were opting for the larger car or SUV. In April 2006 there were about 150,000 vehicles with an engine size between 1700cc and 1900cc. This represents more than five times the number in 1990. Top of the list for emissions are the Land Rover and Range-Rover. One Land Rover Discovery model produces one tonne of carbon dioxide for every 2,518 kilometres. The most energy efficient car on the market in Ireland in 2006 was the Daihatsu Charade 1 litre and the Opel Corsa.[11]

At the moment a lot of attention has been focused on the Toyota Prius. It is a 1.5 litre petrol engine with a dual source of energy, namely a petrol-driven engine and an electric motor. When the car comes to a stop at a traffic light the engine shuts down and the electric motor takes over. The petrol motor does not kick in again until the car builds up speed. The engine is

10. Lynn Sloman, 'Steering Lock' *The Guardian/Society Environment*, 23 March 2006, page 9. Lynn Sloman, *Car Sick: Solutions for our Car-addicted Culture*, Green Books, 2006.
11. Liam Reid, 'SUVs blamed for increasing greenhouse gas emissions', *The Irish Times*, 3 April 2006, page 1.

super efficient and it can travel 1,000 kilometres on a single tank of petrol.

As we have seen, there is the possibility of running cars with hydrogen which is generated by electrolysis. This hydrogen would then be used in a fuel cell in the car to produce electricity to drive the motor which will turn the wheels of the car. The car would also be fitted out with a battery which would allow the fuel cells to operate at a constant rate. This means when the driver wished to accelerate s/he would draw down energy from the battery. When the car is cruising there would be a feedback mechanism which would charge the battery.

On a wider front, we must begin to use cars less. Lynn Sloman, in a new book called *Car Sick: Solutions for our Car-addicted Culture*, makes a number of suggestions which could help ease the congestion on our roads. He quotes a psychologist Jillian Anable who has identified two groups of people who would prefer to use their cars less. He calls them the 'malcontent motorists' and the 'aspiring environmentalists'. With a little creative thinking and planning it should be possible to get these two groups of people to use their car less.

The social scientist Werner Brog carried out an international survey, which included Britain, of the various car journeys that people make. He found out that in four out of ten trips there was an alternative available either to do the trip by bus, train, bicycle or walking. A small improvement in bus services or the provision of a dedicated cycle lane could easily tempt these people out of their cars for almost half their journeys.

He gave the example of the Buckinghamshire Council's effort to encourage people not to travel by car. They began with their own staff and negotiated travel discounts with local transport companies. They installed new cycle lanes and cycle parking depots. They encouraged car-sharing schemes and stopped subsidising parking costs for the employees. They achieved excellent results. Within five years the number of cars driven to work had dropped by 40%.

*Air Travel Causes Massive Pollution*

Flying is a much more polluting form of transport than travelling by bus, train or private car. Aviation is the fastest growing source of carbon dioxide. Burning aviation fuel has what is termed 'radiative force ration' of about 2.7. This means that the full effect of burning aviation fuel is over twice what it would be if the emission took place on the ground through vehicles or power station emissions. The water vapour produced in combustion produce ice crystals in the upper troposphere which trap the earth's heat. Unfortunately, aircraft emissions are currently not included in a country's greenhouse gas emissions allowable under Kyoto. Research carried out at the Tyndall Centre for Climate Prediction and Research concludes that if aviation growth continues at the present rate it could take up the entire carbon emissions for most EU countries allowed under Kyoto.[12]

Air travel causes quite a lot of pollution, especially if it is a long flight. A single jumbo jet flying a return journey from London to Miami in the US each day, releases the equivalent of 520,000 tonnes of carbon dioxide in a single year. A simple way to calculate how much carbon dioxide is produced is just to multiply the distance in miles by 290mg to arrive at the amount of carbon dioxide produced. A number of websites allow a person to offset their carbon burden by supporting green energy or an organisation that plants trees. Two such organisations are www.climatecare.org and www.futureforests.com For example, a one-way flight from London to New York costs one tree, while a return journey to Sydney costs 6 trees. Another way of looking at it is that in carbon dioxide terms the Dublin-Sydney flight is the equivalent of driving around the world 640 times.[13]

The problem is that most analysts believe that, with cheaper fairs from companies like Ryanair, passenger number will rise dramatically during the next two decades. The projected increase in Britain, for example, is from 180 million in 2005 to 496 million

---

12. Shane Coleman, 'Cut-prince air travel may soon cost the earth', *Sunday Tribune*, 12 June 2005, page 16.
13. ibid.

by 2025.[14] Unless the full price of flying, which will include its contribution to global warming, is reflected in the price of the ticket, people will continue flying regardless of the consequences.

Aviation emissions grew by 12% in 2005 and are responsible for 11% of the UK's total greenhouse gas emissions. One of the reasons why air traffic is increasing dramatically both for people and goods is that aviation fuel is not taxed and is VAT free. For this reason, by 2015 planes are expected to double their current contribution of three to five per cent to the global greenhouse effect. Furthermore, airplanes emit nitrogen oxides. These not only contribute to acid rain, but also affect the ozone layer because they are emitted at high altitudes. By 2015, scientists predict that half the annual destruction of the ozone layer will be caused by air traffic alone.

In February 2006, a draft treaty on liberalising aviation between the EU and US was leaked to the press. Article 14 of the proposed 'open skies' treaty waters down any real attempt to stop the exponential growth of air traffic. The US is opposed to having any tax on aviation fuel.[15]

The airline industry has begun to fight back against accusations that flying is environmentally very destructive. Willie Walsh, the chief executive of British Airways, claimed at a conference in Dublin in April 2006 that 'while it is crucial that aviation take action on emissions, the notion that flying is a selfish, antisocial activity that single-handedly threatens planetary catastrophe bears no relation to the evidence'.[16] Andy Harrison, the chief executive of EasyJet, and Michael O'Leary of Ryanair had previously dismissed claims from environmentalists that the growth in air transport was contributing hugely to greenhouse gas emissions. Peter Lockley of the Aviation Environment Foundation, dismissed Walsh's comments by pointing out that

14. George Monbiot, 'An ugly face of ecology', *The Guardian*, 26 April 2005. www.society.guardian.co.uk/26/04/2005> page 1 of 2.
15. Andrew Clark, "Open skies' treaty threatens fight against global warming', *The Guardian*, 20 February 2006, page 1 and 2.
16. Ros Taylor, 'Are aviation pollution claims a flight of fancy?', *The Guardian*, 28 April 2006, page 6.

he willfully ignores the non-carbon dioxide effects of aviation
and the fact that carbon dioxide does more damage when it is injected into the atmosphere at a high altitude. Lockley estimates
that the 'uplift' factor makes emission 2.7 times more damaging,
and in his calculations aviation accounts for 13% of Britain's
greenhouse gas emissions. Because of the proliferation of cheap
flights, Lockley believes that aviation is the fastest growing
source of greenhouse gases. There is an urgent need for systems
that can moderate emissions. The only way to do this is to slow
down the growth of the aviation industry and no one seems
willing to tackle that issue.

The US Air Force are currently testing the possibility of using
alternative fuels in their fleet. In the summer of 2006, the Air
Force plan to test a B-52 bomber with two of its engines running
on jet fuel produced from natural gas. The other six engines will
burn traditional jet fuel. If the test is successful the Air Force
plan to increase their use of synthetic fuel to 100 million gallons
in the next two years.[17]

There is no doubt that the arrival of peak-oil will radically
change the airline business and many of the tourist businesses
that cheap air flights supports.

This will have huge implications for the organisation and
bureaucracy of the Catholic Church because it is so centralised.
Video conferencing will come into its own. Will we be able to
justify Synods where all the bishops have to fly, when there
might be less carbon intensive ways of organising church affairs? And maybe the spin off would be that local churches
would have to engage more whole heartedly in their own affairs
as they determine how to articulate their beliefs, structure their
worship, witness to gospel values and govern themselves, and
that might be a blessing in the long run.

There is one final caution that needs to be stressed. The days
of cheap oil are over and that will affect how we use energy in

17. Thom Shanker, 'Military Plans Tests in Search for an Alternative to
Oil-Based Fuel', *The New York Times*, 14 May 2006,
www.nytimes.com/2006/0514/us/14fuel.html?

the future. The kind of living and working patterns that were built up in the past few decades will not survive in a era when energy will be scarce and expensive. Nothing, not even a hydrogen economy, will allow us to continue using energy in the profligate way we have used petroleum products during the past sixty years. David Fleming makes a very valid point when he writes that 'in a Lean Economy it is appropriateness rather than efficiency that matters'.[18]

18. David Fleming, 'Building a Lean Economy for a fuel-poor future', in *Before the Wells Run Dry*, Richard Douthwaite (ed), 2003, page 104.

# CHAPTER 9

# *How the Churches have Responded to Global Warming*

My argument thus far is that global warming will have, in the main, a negative impact on humankind as well as many other life forms crucial to our survival on earth. We must ask ourselves what steps should the churches take, on a global level as well as at local level, to deal with this threatening reality which is advancing and will bring pain, suffering and death to millions of humans and other creatures.

In order to tackle global warming, the churches should be at the forefront, striving to understand the magnitude of this issue and the urgency with which it must be faced. Peak-oil and global warming are among the most challenging issues humankind has ever faced. Confronting global warming will call for creative leadership in almost every field of human endeavour. If we are to be successful, huge amounts of resources will be needed to confront climate change at every level. People rightly look to the churches for moral and religious support to guide them through this challenging venture

Firstly, we need to understand what is involved in climate change, and what are its consequences. We also need to know what the churches can do as organisations to address it, and what individuals and families can do in their lives to counteract global warming, when motivated by a strong Christian faith. We saw in chapter two that knowledge about climate change and its consequences are available from many scientific bodies and many research institutes. If church leaders wish to genuinely tackle the problem of climate change, they need to seek accurate as well as independent science on ecological issues. It is imperative that they are sure that the research does not come from the perspective of those have vested interests or are poised to make money from one outcome over another.

The hijacking of many academic and government institutions by the corporate world is one of the most pernicious developments in recent decades. In the first chapter of my book *Patenting Life? Stop! Is Corporate Greed Forcing Us to Eat Genetically Engineered Food?*[1] I chart the growth of corporate power since the end of World War II. Transnational Corporations (TNCs) are now among the powerful and influential institutions on earth and, unfortunately, as a result government decisions often favour corporate interests rather than the common good.

Dr Marcia Angell, senior lecturer in social medicine at Harvard University, confirms the above in her book *The Truth about the Drug Companies: How they Deceive Us and What to do about it*. She is critical of the unethical medical trials which pharmaceutical companies from rich countries carry out on poor people in the Majority World. The drugs being tested are not those which might help to address illnesses in poor countries, like malaria. They are geared to Minority World illnesses like heart disease and diabetes. Her key point is simply this: pharmaceutical research is driven too much by profit.[2]

Corporate control can also extend to regulatory agencies. In May 2006, Friends of the Earth Europe claimed that the European Food Safety Authority (EFSA) would not regain public trust unless it disassociated itself from the grip of the biotechnology industry and employed independent scientists instead. Friends of the Earth accused EFSA of three things. The first related to the employment of industry-friendly scientists, the second involved employing scientists with a conflict of interest and, finally, the EFSA had refused to enforce EU law which requires that all the scientists must declare any interest in genetically engineered products.[3]

1. Seán McDonagh, 2003, *Patenting life? Stop! Will Corporate Greed Force us to Eat Genetically Engineered Food?* Dominican Publications, Dublin.
2. Marcia Angell, 'Where our rules don't apply', *The Australian Financial Review*, 18 November 2005, page 6 of the Review.
3. Friends of the Earth Europe press release, 30 May 2006. See www.foreeurope.org/GMOs/publications/ESFAreport.pdf

At this point in time the governments of most of the countries with which I am familiar are cutting back on public science. By this I mean scientific research which takes place at public institutions and which is primarily carried out for the common good rather than to make profits for any corporations. These countries include US, Ireland, the United Kingdom and Australia. Even universities are being colonised by corporations, which will again draw science away from researching issues which would benefit the public and, especially future generations, such as researching potential alternative energy sources. This abandonment of public science will have potentially disastrous consequences for the well being of humans as well as the natural world. Church leaders should champion the cause of public science and should criticise government decisions such as the ones taken in Australia in recent years to cut back on the number of scientists at the Commonwealth Scientific and Industrial Research Oganisation (CSIRO). In 2003, the Labour party opposition spokesperson on science and research, claimed that 850 jobs and A$100 million dollars had been cut from the CSIRO's budget. We must never forget that private research is always oriented to profit. Unless there is publicly supported research, we will not be able to meet the numerous demands of developing a truly sustainable future. The World Council of Churches' document, *Solidarity with Victims of Climate Change* outlines the problem of abandoning public science succinctly: 'Though industry is vitally interested in innovation and will substantially support profit oriented research, the state will need to make sure that research activities can be oriented towards the demands of a sustainable future.'[4]

## The World Council of Churches

When we look to what the churches can do about climate change in the future, it is important to outline what has already been

4. *Solidarity with Victims of Climate Change*, World Council of Churches, 150, route de Ferney, P.O. Box 2100, 1214 Geneva 2, Switzerland, 2002, page 14.

done. It is generally recognised by Christians of all denominations who are committed to working for justice and sustainability that the World Council of Churches (WCC) has given the most courageous leadership of any Christian institution on a wide range of ecological issues, especially, global warming. Over the years, the WCC has developed an extensive body of teaching on global warming. This includes a document published in May 1994 called *Sign of Peril, Test of Faith, Accelerated Climate Change,* and more recently in 2002 a pamphlet, *Solidarity with Victims of Climate Change.*[5]

The WCC has been concerned about environmental issues since the Nairobi Assembly in 1975. As far back as 1988 it sponsored a consultation on global warming in Geneva which was attended by church members, environmental groups, scientists, politicians and theologians. During the subsequent years, the WCC has continued to highlight the importance of developing strategies to combat global warming, firstly because it is a threat to the well-being of God's creation and, secondly as a justice issue between the rich Minority world and poor Majority world because the poor will suffer most from global warming. WCC observers took part in the meetings which led to the adoption of the UN treaty on climate change at the Earth Summit in Rio de Janeiro in 1992.

In the wake of the Rio Earth Summit, the WCC observers presented an assessment of the UN Treaty and made a number of recommendations. Firstly, it felt that it was important to deepen the theological and ethical reflections on climate change. Secondly, it saw the importance of letting people know that responding to climate change would involve profound changes in all spheres of life. Thirdly, the ecological, economic and political aspects of climate change ought to be assessed from a justice perspective, especially in the light of the growing gap between

5. *Sign of Peril, Test of Faith, Accelerated Climate Change,* World Council of Churches, 150, route de Ferney, P.O. Box 2100, 1211 Geneva 2, Switzerland, 1994, and *Solidarity with the Victims of Climate Change, Reflections on the World Council of Churches' Response to Climate Change,* 2002.

the Minority rich world and the Majority poor world. Finally,
the WCC believed that it was crucial to make resources available
to individual churches so that they could use these to develop
educational, advocacy and lifestyle programmes to stablise the
global climate.

*Sign of Peril, Test of Faith* published in 1993 addressed all of
the above issues. Chapter one evaluated the scientific evidence
for global warming and it attempted to predict the future consequences. It accepted that, while there were (are) some uncertainties in the scientific data, it would be irresponsible, in the light of
the 'probably serious consequence for humans and life in general,' to put off making a significant response until all the evidence
showed unequivocally that climate change was happening. The
document supported the adoption of the 'precautionary principle' contained in the Framework Convention on Climate
Change (Article 3.3) This requires political authorities to support strict environmental measures to avoid potentially damaging consequences even in the absence of totally conclusive scientific evidence linking greenhouse gas emissions with global
warming.

Chapter two develops a theological and ethical framework to
help Christians understand the implications of climate change
for their faith. According to the document, these reflections flow
from the basic tenets of the Christian faith. This includes God's
love and concern for creation and the poor of the earth. The
propensity of humans to disobey God's will by inflicting pain on
humans and creation is counterbalanced by the awareness that
God's grace can move peoples' hearts and bring about an ecological conversion. In the context of global warming, true repent-
ance ought to involve a willingness to opt for a new way of life
based on simplicity and sufficiency rather than on the constant
accumulation of material possessions which seems to dominate
contemporary Western culture.

Reflecting on God's care for and sovereignty over creation,
the document reminds Christians that our behaviour is not
merely confined to actions which affect other human beings, but

a violation of creation is also a sin. Of course, a justice-ecologically driven perspective critiques how people in different parts of the world use fossil fuel. One-fifth of the world's population has an insatiable appetite for fossil fuel and is responsible for 85% of the world's greenhouse gas emissions. On the other hand, the poorest 20% of the population needs to increase their use of fossil fuel energy merely to meet and enjoy the basic necessities of life. Aside from the inequities involved in the distribution of global energy resources in the world, present consumption levels of fossil fuels deprive future generations of their fair share of the earth's resources. In summary, the theological and ethical reflections affirm that God loves everything in creation. He calls on human beings to abandon the arrogance and greed that is harming the earth and endangering creation's future.

Chapter three looks at what a positive response to global warming might mean for the various sectors of society. It attempts to spell out what might be involved for industry, and especially transnational corporations, as they trade in goods and services around the world. The document is adamant that any comprehensive response to global warming will involve profound changes at a social, political and economic level in every part of the Minority world.

Chapter four discusses how countries might reduce their output of greenhouse gases through developing a realistic timetable which would involve the carrot and stick approach of incentives to change and penalties for not changing. This chapter and following ones recognise that the response from the affluent Minority world and the rich in the Majority world will need to be different. People have a right to the provision of adequate food and the basic necessities of life, but they do not have a right to waste energy or abuse the earth. Governments and industry must pursue policies which promote energy efficiency and accelerate the shift from fossil fuel to energy use derived from renewable sources – wind, wave, tidal, solar, micro-hydro and biomass.

Chapter six raises the crucial question: Can the targets for

emissions be met within the present global socio-political system where economic growth is extolled as the panacea for all
problems, especially overcoming poverty in the Majority world
and unemployment in the Minority world? The document has
challenged the validity of the growth model by pointing out that
unlimited economic growth is manifestly impossible in a finite
world. It also challenges people in the Minority world to live
more simply so that energy will be available for the poor who
need it badly just to improve their basic standard of living. The
drafters of the document were not naïve. They recognise that
governments are much more responsive to the vested interests
of powerful economic groups who are committed to the present
growth-oriented system for as long as they can make profits
from it.

Chapter seven argues that reducing the threat of global
warming will require a new vision of what constitutes the good
life. The good life today is caught up with wealth, ownership of
property, a huge carbon footprint and a concern for external ap-
pearances. Transforming this vision will not be easy. The WCC
vision in relation to global warming is an attempt to transform
our relationships with other human beings and motivate us to
live in harmony with the rest of creation.

Chapters eight and nine examine the potential role of the
churches in addressing the crisis of human-induced climate
change. This sketches the broad contours of a spirituality based
on pursuing global justice, peace and integrity of creation. In
line with the churches' prophetic vocation which is to denounce
evil and empower Christians to seek the path of reconciliation
and harmony, the report insists that the churches must actively
campaign on global warming in co-operation with independent
environmental organisations such as Friends of the Earth. The
crucial question of wealthy lifestyles in the Minority world is
also addressed. Are not the comforts which many people enjoy
today, and consider essential for their wellbeing, a careless exploitation of nature and unsustainable in the long-term? The
authors remind contemporary Christians that their Christian

ancestors lived simple but fulfilling lives and that too is possible today.

I have dwelt at length on *Sign of Peril, Test of Faith* because I believe that the methodology used and the message it proposes are as relevant to Catholics as they are to other Christian Churches. Its analysis of global warming is competent, both from a scientific and a theological perspective, and its recommendations are appropriate and well-thought out at both the global and local levels. It suggests a viable programme for action as a way of responding to one of the most important contemporary ethical questions.

In March 1996, the then President of the Pontifical Council for Justice and Peace, Cardinal Roger Etchegaray wrote to the Presidents of the Episcopal Conferences of industrial countries and acknowledged that the World Council of Churches had taken a leading role in drawing the attention of its member churches to the relationship between climate change and human activity. He encouraged local churches to examine ways in which they could co-operate with any WCC-inspired initiative in their country. Unfortunately, little happened then or is happening now.

In 2002, the WCC followed up with another excellent document on climate change entitled *Solidarity with Victims of Climate Change*. This document pointed out that the extreme weather conditions caused by climate change are costing a fortune. Insurance companies claim that very soon the bill will mount up to $300 billion annually. Countries in the Majority world will be the most vulnerable. The document recognises that the Kyoto Protocol is only a beginning, because the scientists on the Intergovernmental Panel on Climate Change (IPCC) were calling for a 60% to 80% reduction in greenhouse gas emissions by the year 2050, whereas the reduction for industrialised countries in the protocol only reached 5.2%. The document does point out that, with the vast array of technologies and policy measures on energy supply and demand, the targets are achievable, if there is strong political leadership.[6] On pages 13 and 14 the document

6. *Solidarity with Victims of Climate Change: Reflections on the World*

discusses the World Trade Oorganisation Conference in Doha (November 2001). They make the valid point that it is almost impossible to insert binding ecological criteria into the WTO. 'The system is basically incapable of integrating the environmental dimension. Though market mechanisms are to be affirmed for the promotion of the exchange of goods, they are unable to set the scales and limits which must be respected for the sake of the environment. For measures containing the dynamism of the market, the role of the state is indispensable.'[7]

The WTO is a relatively young organisation, set up in 1994. One would have rightly expected that it should have factored into its remit on trade environmental considerations. For example, beef produced by destroying rainforests is as legitimate an object of trade as beef produced on grass lands in an environmentally friendly way as far as the WTO is concerned. Ecological concerns do not enter into its policies of regulating world trade. The WTO is also very secretive in its decision making processes and has given no space whatsoever to independent non-government organisations.

In contrast, in the 1980s the World Bank and even the International Monetary Fund (IMF) began to talk about the importance of protecting vital ecosystems such as tropical forests and coral reefs in the past few years and of involving non-government organisations in their consultations. The World Trade Organisation emerged from the 8th Round of the GATT which began in the mid-1980s. The multinational corporations now felt that they needed a strong trading body to protect their interests especially in the area of patents, financial services etc. This is the reason why the US and the EU gave their *imprimatur* to the WTO. Right though out the period in which the Uruguay Round was being negotiated, there was much talk about the deteriorating global situation. The United Nations produced the Brundtland Report, published as *Our Common Future* in 1987,

Council of Churches' Response to Climate Change, page 11.
7. ibid pages 14.

and the Earth Summit took place in Rio de Janeiro.[8] At that event, politicians made fine speeches about protecting the global commons. Yet the WTO felt free to exclude ecological considerations from its mandate to mediate global trade. This shows that, despite all the fine rhetoric, politicians have very little interest in addressing environmental concerns. Peter Sutherland, who managed the transition from GATT to the WTO, was aware that addressing long-term environmental issues should take precedence over promoting a so-called free-trade regime globally.

To return to the WCC 2002 document, it is an accurate and bleak assessment of the current ecological situation. It states that 'destructive processes have continued and are continuing. Change is unlikely to occur through persuasion. It may take place as the dysfunctioning of the system becomes more and more obvious. It will be accompanied by upheavals and suffering.' The pamphlet ends with a brief theological reflection which is very appropriate in the current context. 'There is no guarantee that resistance will be crowned by success. The future is unknown. There is a distinct possibility that 'love will grow cold' (Mt 24:12). It is essential that our love does not depend on the assurances of success. Faith, hope and love abide, says Paul. Love transcends the limits of this life. The hope for God's absolute future is the ultimate motivation of love.'[9]

One of the people who has done most to raise awareness of global warming in the churches is Dr David G. Hallman. He is the Climate Change Programme Co-ordinator of the World Council of Churches. At a conference on climate change, which was organised by Catholic EarthCare Australia in Canberra in November 2005, he described the extensive work of the WCC worldwide. It is an impressive list of accomplishments which includes the following:

- The Pacific Conference of Churches and the WCC Pacific Office are active in helping churches throughout the island

8. *Our Common Future*, The World Commission on Environment and Development, Oxford University Press, 1987.
9. ibid, page 26.

states (in the Pacific) address the serious threat that climate change poses to their societies;

- In India, the WCC has helped to support a network called the Indian Network on Ethics and Climate Change which involves Christians (both Catholics and Protestants) working with environmental and development organisations to engage people in many different regions of the country on the issues regarding climate change;
- The European Christian Environment Network has had an active climate change programme for several years as have some of its national members including the Christian Ecology Link in the United Kingdom;
- The All Africa Council of Churches has been a partner with the WCC in workshops in the past which have been focused in communities on the links between climate change and water issues;
- The Latin America Council of Churches is working with other groups in civil society on an environmental citizenship project that includes a developed faith-based curriculum on environmental concerns for use in seminaries and parishes;
- In the USA, the National Religious Partnership on the Environment (NRPE) has had a long-term programme of education and advocacy on climate change. The NRPE includes the US Evangelical Environmental Network, and the Coalition on Environment and Jewish Life:
- Canadian Churches collaborate ecumenically in a coalition called Kairos Canada which has an active climate change programme.[10]

*The Catholic Church*

In contrast to the WCC, which has extensive teaching on many aspects of the ecological crisis, Catholic teaching on the same subject either from the Papal Magisterium or Bishops Conferences is pretty meagre. In 2002, Sister Marjore Keenan wrote a book drawing together Papal teaching on the ecological crisis. Her

---

10. www.catholicearthcareoz.net homepage / Conference 2005.

book was published by the Pontifical Council For Justice and
Peace and is entitled, *Care for Creation: Human Activity and the
Environment*. While she has done an excellent job in bringing this
teaching together in a single volume, it is still a rather slim one.
If one were to bring together the recent teachings on sexual matters within the Catholic Church, I think it would be a much heftier
set of volumes.

Chapter ten of the *Compendium of the Social Doctrine of the
Church* is devoted to safeguarding the environment.[11] It is one of
the slimmest chapters in the book, a mere 15 pages. Chapter 6 on
human work has 27 pages. While there is much good material in
chapter 10, I would argue that it is the weakest chapter in the
entire book. Nine articles are devoted to biotechnology and only
one paragraph to the destruction of biodiversity. The chapter
does not highlight the magnitude of the ecological crisis nor the
urgency with which it must be faced in order to ensure a future
for the peoples of the earth and many other creatures. The important talks given by Pope John Paul II on the urgency of the ecological crisis and the need for an 'ecological conversion' are not
found in this book. Why?

In a public audience on 17 January 2001, Pope John Paul II
said: 'If we scan the regions of our planet, we immediately see
that humanity has disappointed God's expectations. Man, especially in our time, has without hesitation devastated wooded
plains and valleys, polluted waters, disfigured the earth's habitat, made the air unbreathable, disturbed the hydrogeological
and atmospheric spheres and turned luxuriant areas into deserts
and undertaken forms of unrestrained industrialisation, humili-
ating the flower-garden of the universe, to use the image of
Dante Alighieri (Paradiso, XX11, 151). We must therefore encourage and support the 'ecological conversion' that in recent
decades has made humanity more sensitive to the catastrophe to
which it has been heading. Man is no longer the Creator's 'steward', but an autonomous despot, who has finally beginning to

11. *Compendium of the Social Doctrine of the Church*, Veritas Publications,
Dublin, 2004.

understand that he must stop at the edge of the abyss.'[12] In this talk the late pope captures the magnitude of contemporary eco-logical issues, the urgency of facing them and the need for an 'ecological conversion'. Why it was not included in the *Compend-ium of The Social Doctrine of the Church* baffles me.

Given the paltry amount of teaching on ecological issues in general, it should come as no surprise that there is hardly any teaching from the Papal Magisterium or Bishops Conferences on global warming, even though this is the most serious ecological issue facing the planet now and during the next fifty years. One of the first places where there is a reference to global warming in Papal teaching is in the 1990 document on ecology, *Peace with God the Creator; Peace with all Creation*. The sixth paragraph of the document lumps together global warming and the destruction of the ozone layer by CFCs. The documents states that 'The gradual depletion of the ozone layer and the related 'green-house effect' have now reached crisis proportions …' While CFCs are global warming gases, the depletion of the ozone layer and global warming are two entirely different things. This, of course, reiterates the point I have made on page 152, the need for moral teaching on any ecological issues to be grounded in accu-rate science.

A small number of Episcopal Conferences have reflected on global warming and climate change. A number of Catholic theo-logians have also written on the issue. The numbers are very small when one thinks about the urgency of the issue. This book is an attempt to develop a theological response to global warm-ing from a combination of some traditional and contemporary moral principles. As I have said, there is a brief mention of global warming in the newly published *Compendium of the Social Doctrine of the Church*. No 470 of the *Compendium* states: 'Every economic activity making use of natural resources must also be concerned with safeguarding the environment and should fore-see the costs involved, which are an essential part of the actual

12. Pope John Paul II, 'God made man the steward of creation', *L'Osservatore Romano*, 24 January 2001, page 11.

cost of economic activity.' In this context, 'one considers relations between human activity and climate change which, given their extreme complexity, must be opportunely and constantly monitored at the scientific, political and juridical, national and international levels. The climate is a good that must be protected' and reminds consumers and those engaged in industrial activity to develop a greater sense of responsibility for their behaviour.[13]

These few sentences can form the basis of a Catholic response to global warming and climate change.

### Climate Change and Common Good

Returning to the above paragraph in the *Compendium* which states that 'climate is a good that must be protected', concern for the 'common good' has traditionally been at the heart of Catholic moral and social teaching. In an extensive reflection on the 'common good' the *Compendium* goes on to state that 'the common good that people seek and attain in the formation of social communities is the guarantee of their personal, familial and associative good' (numbers 61, 164, 165, 168, 170).

Contemporary moral theologians like David Hollenbach SJ have written about the difficulties of speaking about the common good in a pluralist society where there still is some memory of the authoritarian urge, both in the religious sphere and the ideologically driven political sphere, to impose on one segment of society values and perspectives that are perceived as common good by only one element in that society. Particularly in the US context, but more and more globally, cultural differences make discussion of the common good difficult. Many argue that 'tolerance of difference' rather than the common good has become the highest social aspiration in the US. Hollenbach is very aware that an adequate response to the major social and political problems of today needs moral vision with more energy behind it than the tolerance culture can create on its own.

Surprisingly, he does not include the environment as one of these challenges which he outlines. Later in his book he does

---

13. ibid, No 470.

state that 'Americans see a link between their own good as a nation and the good of people in other countries where this link is direct and obvious. An example of this kind of direct linkage is the need for environmental protection, a good that is indivisible in the long term because all countries are mutually dependent on the biophysical environment that knows no boundaries.'[14]

What the *Compendium*, with the exception of Number 170, and almost all Catholic Social Teaching overlooks, is that life-giving human social relations are always embedded in vibrant and sustainable ecosystems. Anything that negatively impacts on ecosystems or alters the equilibrium of the biosphere, such as global warming, is a disruption of the common good in a most fundamental way – especially if it creates negative irreversible changes. Even Hollenbach's nuanced presentation of the common good tends to forget the fact that the destruction of creation undermines the common good.

This is exactly what climate change is doing. To sum up the challenge briefly: In January 2004, Sir David King, the chief scientist to the British Government, stated that climate change was the most serious issue facing the human community. Therefore in his view, US climate policy is a bigger threat to the world than terrorism is. 'As a consequence of continued warming, millions more people around the world may in future be exposed to the risk of hunger, drought, flooding and debilitating diseases such as malaria.'[15] Given the deleterious consequence of climate change on every human society and ecosystem, it seems natural that we should use the common good argument to bolster a variety of actions, at an individual, national and planetary level, that will be necessary in order to halt runaway climate change.

The *Compendium* does open up another avenue closely allied to issues of the 'common good' by its support in number 468 for

---

14.David Hollenback SJ, 2002, *The Common Good and Christian Ethics*, Cambridge University Press, Washington DC, page 50.
15. Steve Connor, 'US climate policy is a bigger threat to world than terrorism', *The Independent*, 9 January 2004, page 1.

'the right to a safe and healthy environment'. Pope John Paul II referred to this emerging juridical consensus in an address to the European Commission and Court of Human Rights in Strasbourg on 8 October 1988. The Pope was aware that the environmental justice movements and human rights movements are increasingly applying a rights-based strategy to confront global devastation. This particular right is seen within the wider expansion of the notion of human rights in the past two decades. These include the right to an adequate living standard, the right to education, the right to food and water, the right to adequate provisions for remaining healthy and the right to housing and work.

The right to a healthy environment requires a healthy human habitat. This precludes anything that might damage the life sustaining processes of the planet which includes access to clean water, fresh air and fertile soils free from toxins or hazards which would threaten human well-being. If, as we know, global warming is going to make the climatic conditions for the earth and humans extremely unpleasant, then campaigns to promote action on global warming could be fought under the banner of a right to a stable climate.

In his book *The Minding of Planet Earth*, Cardinal Cahal Daly calls attention to the World Charter for Nature which was presented to the United Nations on 28 September 1982. The aim of the Charter was to protect 'essential ecological and life support systems and … the diversity of life forms'. It is akin to the right to a safe environment but expands the focus to include other species as well as human. The Cardinal rightly points out that the recommendations in the Charter are so nebulous that they do not amount to much. They must be revisited and given more teeth.

*Intergenerational Justice*
Another source for shaping a theology and morality to underpin action on global warming comes from a concern for intergenerational justice. Traditional ethical concerns normally dealt with the impact of our behaviour on individuals or communities in

the here-and-now or the immediate future. This is no longer an adequate framework because this generation, through its powerful technologies, is bringing about massive changes to the fabric of the earth, which will affect in a negative way every succeeding generation of humans and other creatures. The basic principle which arises from this ethical concern is that future generations have the right to inherit a world as fertile and as beautiful as the one which we inhabit. This new moral context is recognised in number 470 of the *Compendium of the Social Doctrine of the Church*. It states: 'From a moral perspective based on equity and intergenerational solidarity, it will be necessary to continue, through the contribution of the scientific community, to identify new sources of energy, develop alternative sources and increase the security level of nuclear energy.' This is clear from chapter four where I argued that nuclear power is not the solution to global warming.

Concern for future generations would also help us counteract the following attitude which is prevalent among many people, especially politicians and bureaucrats: 'If something is not going to happen on my watch, then I'll leave it to my successor to deal with it, even though I know what I am doing now will exacerbate the problem and maybe create a situation which may be irreversible.'

In response to this attitude, the church needs to develop its teaching on sustainability and on the 'precautionary principle'. We need to reformulate the idea of sustainable development which was the bedrock of the Brundtland Report published as *Our Common Future* in 1987. It defined sustainable development as seeking 'to meet the needs and aspirations of the present without compromising the ability to meet those of the future.' Then it went on to affirm that 'far from requiring the cessation of economic growth, it recognises that the problems of poverty and underdevelopment cannot be solved unless we have a new era of growth in which developing countries play a large role and reap large benefits.'[16] Almost 20 years later any ecological

16. *Our Common Future*, op. cit., page 40.

evaluation of the impact of economic growth on either the Irish economy, which was in the doldrums when the report was written, or more especially the two digit annual growth of the Chinese economy, should make it absolutely clear that the western, oil-dependent kind of growth which China and India are now pursuing are environmentally unsustainable as well as devastating to the entire planet.

The WCC document, *Solidarity with Victims of Climate Change* is quite insightful in its analysis of the effects of untrammelled economic growth. It says that 'as we seek to re-define the concept of "sustainable development" this hard reality (of planetary limits) needs to be taken into account. Increasingly, the need to resist degradation and to limit its effects will have to be recognised as an important dimension of sustainability. The term development has no longer the connotation of improving life conditions and eventually leading to a "better world". The emphasis will be much more on increasing the capacity to survive in deteriorating life conditions.'[17]

We need to be reminded that the earth is finite and that we must live in a way that is fair and just to future generations of humans and other creatures.

The precautionary principle is another moral principle which is mentioned in Number 469 of the *Compendium of the Social Teachings of the Church*. This document presents the 'precautionary principle' in the context of making practical decisions about the impact of an action on human health or environmental well-being when contradictory scientific opinions are being offered. The texts states that in such a situation 'it may be appropriate to base evaluations on the precautionary principle, which does not mean applying rules but certain guidelines aimed at managing a situation of uncertainty.' The text implies that it is useful in dealing with difficult ethical situations.

However, the presentation of the precautionary principle as not so much a set of rules but 'certain guidelines' leaves open the

17. *Solidarity with Victims of Climate Change: Reflections on the World Council of Churches' Response to Climate Change*, 2002, page 15.

possibility for widening out its scope to judge and challenge any kind of policies, especially economic ones, which may bring short-term economic benefits to a few at the cost of permanent ecological damage to an ecosystem or habitat. The *Compendium* does acknowledge this in Number 470 when it states that 'programmes of economic development must carefully consider the need to respect the integrity and cycles of nature because natural resources are limited and some are not renewable'. Once again there is an assumption that this principle applies to a local situation. Now it must be applied in a situation where human activity is adversely changing climatic conditions for this and future generations.

The US Conference of Catholic Bishops introduced the virtue of prudence into their reflections on climate change. The bishops wrote that:

> This virtue is not only a necessary one for individuals in leading morally good lives, but is also vital to the moral health of the larger community. Prudence is intelligence applied to our actions. It allows us to discern what constitutes the common good in a given situation. Prudence requires a deliberate and reflective process that aids in the shaping of the community's conscience. Prudence not only helps us identify the principles at stake in a given issue, but also moves us to adopt courses of action to protect the common good. Prudence is not, as popularly thought, simply a cautious and safe approach to decisions. Rather it is a thoughtful, deliberate and reasoned basis for taking or avoiding action to achieve a moral good.[18]

The bishops are very clear that prudence is not meant to inhibit action nor promote a business-as-usual approach. It challenges people, especially those in positions of authority, to reflect on the current scientific data on global warming. But prudence will not allow us simply to nod our heads in agreement with those who

18. United States Conference of Catholic Bishops, *Global Climate Change, A Plea for Dialogue, Prudence and the Common Good*, 15 June 2002. See www.usccb.org/sdwp/ejp/bsstatement.html

are predicting that climate change will have massive and general negative consequences for the future. Prudence, properly understood, calls for courageous action when faced with a major social or ecological problem. In the case of global warming, prudence will demand radical actions to curb greenhouse gas emissions and some of the recommendations will call for fairly major sacrifices from this generation. But the stakes are so high that no other course of action would be prudent.

We also need to understand the nature of irreversible ecological damage and its implications for future generations. The potential damage from global warming to the earth and the peoples of the earth is enormous. Unless this and the next generation stabilise the emissions of global warming gases, then the consequences are inevitable and irreversible in geological time. It is an extraordinary and awesome moment in human and earth affairs that the behaviour of one or two generations can have such a profound and irreversible impact, not just on human history, but on the planet as well.

*Preferential Option for the Poor*
Another principle which is helpful in the search for an ecological theology is the preferential option for the poor. This is a relatively recent moral principle which emerged, especially in Latin America, during the second part of the 20th century. It is now enshrined in Catholic Social Teaching. It challenges individuals and societies to examine ethical and economic choices from the point of view of how they will affect poor people, not just in their locality, but globally as well.[19] Will these ethical and economic choices enhance the life of the poor or further impoverish them? Global warming will have a devastating impact on the poor as these few examples will illustrate.

One of the abiding tragedies and ironies in reflecting on global warming is that the poor, who have contributed least to it, will suffer most. The World Council of Churches' document on climate change, *Sign of Peril, Test of Faith*, includes a chart on page

---

19. *Compendium of the Social Doctrine of the Church*, number 59.

11 which attempts to calculate emissions of carbon dioxide from various countries between 1800 and 1988. According to the chart, North America contributed 32.2%, Europe's contribution was 26.1%, Latin America was 3.8% and China was 5.5%. China's carbon dioxide emissions have grown enormously since. (It is now estimated that by 2025 China will have overtaken the US as the top emitter of Greenhouse gases if the present trend of fossil fuel use continues.[20] Archbishop Desmond Tuut, in the foreword to the recent publication *Africa – Up in Smoke?*, states the problem of global warming very succinctly: 'The World's wealthiest countries have emitted more than their fair share of greenhouse gases. Resultant floods, droughts and other climate change impacts continue to fall disproportionately on the world's poorest people and countries, many of which are in Africa.'[21]

The church community and all humankind need to respond to the plight of the poor. *Solidarity* was a concept much beloved of Pope John Paul II. In his Encyclical *Sollicitudo Rei Socialis* (Concern for Social Realities 1987, No 38) he describes solidarity 'not as a feeling of vague compassion or shallow distress at the misfortunes of so many people, both near and far. On the contrary, it is a firm and persevering determination to commit oneself to the common good: that is to say the good of all and of each individual, because we are all really responsible for all' (par 37). In the context of the deepening ecological crisis, solidarity acknowledges that we are increasingly bound together as members of the earth community. In her overview of the statements on ecology from the Holy See, Sister Marjorie Keenan writes that the 'concept of solidarity also extends to nature'.[22]We

20. Michael McCarthy, 'The China Crisis'. *The Independent*, 19 October 2005, page 1.
21. *Africa – Up in Smoke?* (2005). The second report of the Working Group on Climate Change and Development, written and compiled by Andrew Simms, policy director of the New Economics Foundation, 3 Jonathan Street, London SE11 5NH.
22. Sister Margorie Keenan, RSHM, *From Stockholm to Johannesburg*, Pontifical Council for Justice and Peace, Vatican City, 2002, page 38.

are responsible for the well being of the poor and all creation. Both these destinies are intertwined. We will either bequeath to the next generation of all life a fruitful, beautiful and vibrant planet for the well being of all creatures or all future generations will be diminished. In such a barren and polluted world future generations will be forced to live amid the ruins, not merely of the technological world, but of the natural world itself.

*Concern for the wider Earth Commnity*

Another element in the moral framework is a concern for the wider earth community. The wider earth community encompasses all life. This perspective on life has only begun to emerge in recent times. Unfortunately, it is not completely central to the teachings of Vatican Congregations or Councils. Part of the reason for this is the almost absolute priority which we have given to the human. This is clearly expressed in the *Compendium* number 171 quoting Vatican II *Gaudium et Spes* number 69: 'God destined the earth and all it contains for all men and all peoples so that all created things would be shared fairly by all mankind under the guidance of justice tempered by charity.' Today moral theologians are arguing that other creatures have more than just instrumental value for humans as sources of food, clothing and medicine. The wider earth community is not recognised as having intrinsic value in itself. Anyone who studies nature knows that God has taken as much care in creating other species, especially the smaller creatures, as he has in creating the humans. After all, humans only emerged over 2 million years ago. This is merely the flick of an eyelid in the 3.7 billion years of life on earth. God loves other creatures and we humans are linked to them through close genetic bonding. Given our present ecological challenges, either the whole biosphere will prosper or we all go down together.

Unfortunately, very few moralists have made the paradigm shift to a less anthropocentric view of creation. Even David Hollenbach operates out of a homocentric position with regard to nature. This is clear in his reflection on what the Catholic understanding of common good might offer to the wider human community. He writes that the distinctive Catholic contribution 'could be a vision of social solidarity and justice based on the equal dignity of every member of the human race.'[23] True the environment figures much more prominently in his work than in the documents of Vatican II, but he still finds it difficult to break out of an exclusively human perspective.

Things may be changing, albeit slowly. In a recent reflection on the first part of Psalm 135, Pope Benedict XVI said that 'the first visible sign of this divine love is found in creation ... Even before discovering God who reveals himself in history, there is the cosmic revelation open to all, offered to all humanity by the one Creator of all.' The Pope continued: 'There exists, therefore, a divine message, secretly inscribed in creation and a sign of *hesed*, or loving fidelity of God who gives his creatures being and life, water and food.'[24]

*Preaching the Gospel of Life*
The churches' response to the destruction of entire ecosystems and the extinction of an enormous number of creatures should be to preach and embody a Gospel of Life. This will involve challenging some of the most powerful business groups in the world today. In Britain, Sir Digby Jones, the Director General of the Confederation of British Industry (CBI) criticised the British government's modest targets to reduce carbon dioxide emissions as 'risking the sacrifice of UK jobs on the altar of green credentials'.[25] What Sir Digby Jones really fears is a reduction in profits for the members of the CBI. By his comments he appears to put short-term profits ahead of the long-term well-being of the planet. Religious leaders are remiss in their prophetic ministry if they are unwilling to challenge such ultimately destructive policies.

---

23. David Hollenbach, op. cit., page 242.
24. Fides services, 7 November 2005.
25. Andrew Taylor, 'Jobs warning over touch move on emissions', *Financial Times*, 20 January 2004.

*Commitment to Bio-responsibility*

Throughout this book I argue that global warming is having and will continue to have a devastating effect on the living world. In Genesis 2:15 we are called to care for our planet. The destruction of species, which is happening through global warming, is having a devastating impact on the living world. For too long our moral compass was underpinned by the doctrine of the Greek philosopher Protagoras who proclaimed that 'man is the measure of all things which are, that they are so, and of all things which are not, that they are not'.[26] Humans are now called to Bio-responsibility. This means extending the covenant of justice which is found in Genesis 9:12-17 to include all life-forms as God's beloved creatures and as expressions of God's presence, wisdom, power and glory. This is expressed beautifully in the publication *The Gift of Water – A Statement Endorsed by Bishops of the Murray-Darling Region* in Australia. The text states: 'According to St Thomas and St Bonaventure the diversity of species represents the wonder and beauty of God that transcends any one creature. God's creatures express and represent the Trinity. They are not simply there for human use, but have their own dignity, value and integrity. Such a view challenges the destruction of species and their habitat in the modern era.'[27]

As a result of insights gained from ecological theology, we Christians must realise that ethical behaviour must no longer be confined solely to our relationship with God and other human beings. It must also extend and include our relationship with all creation. We must reformulate the Vatican II sentiment, which has been the teaching of the church since Patristic times, by saying that 'the goods of the earth are meant for all the people of the world and all the creatures of the world'.

---

26. Robert Barry Leal, *The Environment and Christian Faith: An Introduction to Ecotheology*, St Paul's Publications; 60-70 Broughton Rd. PO Box 906, Stratfield, NSW, 2004, page 15

27. *The Gift of Water: A Statement from Catholic Earthcare Australia endorsed by Bishops of the Murray-Darling Basin*, 2004 www.catholicearthcareoz.net

*Prophetic Role*

We must also consider the prophetic duty of the churches with regard to global warming. A bible-based moral theology emphasises the two aspects of the prophetic role of the church. Firstly, having weighed up all the issues involved, the church must challenge individuals and institutions which are primarily responsible for global warming to change their affluent lifestyles and their profligate use of energy. I find the US Bishops' statement, which I referred to above, lacking in courage. The bishops state that, while recognising the importance of international solidarity in addressing problems like global warming, they are unwilling to recommend that the US government sign up to the Kyoto Protocol. 'Without endorsing the specifics of these agreements and processes, we Catholic bishops acknowledge the development of these international negotiations and hope they and other future efforts can lead to just and effective progress.'[28] This statement is unhelpful; it lacks clear judgement on what is involved. When dealing with human abortion or experiments on human embryos they do not hesitate in recommending courses of action, even when it is supporting one side in the current US body politic. Even now, with only a rise of 0.63 degrees celsius, the impact on areas as diverse as the Arctic, Antarctic and Sub-Saharan Africa has been enormous. The current projection that the average temperature of the earth will rise 3 degrees celsius at the lower register is truly cause for alarm. If, at the outer limits, the temperature increased by 11 degrees celsius over the next few hundred years or so, it would be a catastrophe for every species on earth including our own.

Given the unwillingness of the Bush administration to do anything significant about climate change, the Catholic Church in the US should not remain silent about this. The issue is so important that the Christian churches must show the necessary courage to challenge vested interests in the name of the poor, in the name of future generations and the wounded earth commu-

---

28. United States Conference of Catholic Bishops, *Global Climate Change*, op. cit.

nity. What would the Prophet Amos say to the rich who are destroying the earth for all future generations? He who thundered
against the lifestyle of the women of Samaria whose extravagant
demands oppressed the needy and crushed the poor (Amos 4:1)
would not hesitate to challenge President George W. Bush's in-
transigence on climate change. And what would he say to
Catholic bishops in the richest country on earth who are unwilling to raise a challenge on behalf of life?

Secondly, the prophetic mission of the church challenges the
Catholic community to provide space within its ranks where
people can live in a much less carbon-intensive way and yet
have a decent standard of living.

In June 2006, Cardinal Cheong Jin-suk of Seoul, Korea issued
a pastoral letter challenging Korean Catholics to live the gospel
in a 'sustaining and renewable way'. The Cardinal wrote that
the ecological crisis, which the world is facing today, is of crucial
relevance to the future and that the church should take a leadership role. The 16-page pastoral letter concentrated on the use of
fossil fuel energy, threats to biodiversity, the effects of petrochemical agriculture and the shortage and unsustainable distribution of food. The letter made a number of practical suggestions about how people might begin to take ecological issues
more seriously. These include making ecological education
more available for young people through summer camps. The
clergy need to be educated as well if any of these initiatives are
to prosper in the next decade.[29]

*Church in Australia has Responded to Environmental Degradation*
The church in Australia is the only Catholic Church in the
English speaking world which has taken the environmental crisis seriously. In 2002, the Social Justice Statement focused on the
environment. The statement felt that 'possibly the most disturb-
ing environmental phenomenon of recent times is the threat of
global warming. The majority of environmental scientists agree

29. Cardinal Cheong Jin-suk, 'Gospel call to live ecological life: Korean
Cardinal', *OnlineCatholic*, 27 June 2006.

that the release of greenhouse gas emissions into the atmosphere is threatening to change our climate patterns, raise sea levels and harm life on earth.

'As the worst emitters per person of greenhouse gases on the planet, Australians are particularly challenged in justice to reflect on the plight of our Pacific island neighbours. The cry of the seven million inhabitants of these beautiful islands, including Tuvalu, Kiribati, Palau, Tonga, Nauru and the Cook islands, who fear that their lands will be battered and submerged by rising sea levels and changing weather patterns, require us to take immediate measures to reduce greenhouse gas emissions.'[30]

The impact of global warming on the Great Barrier Reef is discussed in *Let the Many Coastlands be Glad: A Pastoral Letter on the Great Barrier Reef* by the Catholic Bishops of Queensland. The bishops tell us that 'the Reefs are now warmer than 100 years ago because the temperature has risen by 0.6 degrees celsius. ... corals live in a very narrow 'envelope' of thermal tolerance where temperatures of only 1 degree celsius above normal summer conditions cause them to stress (bleach). When exposed to these conditions over a long period, corals die.

'In 1998 and again in 2002, coral bleaching demonstrably occurred across most of the Great Barrier Reef, killing up to 90 per cent of the corals on some reefs. Coral change scientists report that these events are a wake-up call as climate change is likely to make such happenings more frequent and severe.'[31]

The pastoral letter went on to acknowledge some of the sacrifices which have been made but as they are aware of the seriousness of the problem, the bishops call for action both from the State Government and from individuals to protect the reef.

In November 2005, Catholic Earth Care Australia organised an international conference on climate change in Canberra.

---

30. 2002 Social Justice Sunday Statement, www.catholiceaerethcareoz.net
31. *Let the Many Coastlands Be Glad! A Pastoral Letter on the Great Barrier Reef*, by the Catholic Bishops of Queensland, June 8, 2004, page 20. available from Catholic Earthcare Australia. www.catholicearthcare-oz.net

Bishop Christopher, Chair of Catholic Earthcare Australia and a member of the Bishops Committee for Justice, Development, Ecology and Peace, presented a document on climate change to the conference called *Climate Change: Our Responsibility to Sustain God's Earth*. The document opens with clear acceptance that 'rapid climate change as a result of human activity is now recognised by the global scientific community as a reality'.[32] The document went on to say that 'the web of life on earth is under threat from accelerated climate change. That web compares to a seamless garment and it needs the application of a consistent ethic to protect it, one that considers life now and in the future, and ranges from protection of the unborn child to cherishing the diversity of species. Life is one, and human well-being is at its base interwoven with all life on earth and the rhythms of its systems. The sufferings of one part means that all creation groans, and rapid global climate change dramatically displays that suffering.'[33]

Competent scientists spoke at the Conference attended by 500 people. Dr Janette Lindesay was very clear that climate change is disrupting many of the crucial life support systems on the planet, including the hydrological cycle and the great currents of the oceans. The disruption is becoming evident with increased floods and droughts, extreme weather conditions and rising ocean levels, and the possible diminution or even cessation of the Gulf Stream which provides Western Europe with the equivalent of one million power stations. It is also leading to many more typhoons in Asia. During a two and a half week visit to the Philippines in late July 2006, three typhoons passed close to the Philippines and brought torrential rain and mudslides, loss of life and environmental destruction.

Dr Brendan Mackey, another Canberra climate-scientist, also insisted that, while climate change can be extremely complex given all the factors which must be taken account of, neverthe-

---

32. *Climate Change: Our Responsibility to Sustain God's Earth*, Catholic Earthcare Australia, 2005, page 4.
33. ibid page 7.

less there is a consensus among the scientific community that it is happening and that unless greenhouse gas levels are reduced the impact of climate change on individuals and communities in the future will be disastrous. Both he and Dr Lindesay pointed out that there has been a huge increase in information in the academic world in the past few years and that now they are able to model how climate change might affect a particular geographical area, like for example, the Murray-Daring.

Fr Michael McKenzie, a priest from the island of Kibiriti in the Pacific, gave personal testimony on the impact of climate change and the rising oceans on the island people where he lives. This was a most poignant presentation because it moved from the scientific language of the morning and showed on a DVD the direct impact of rising sea levels and tidal surge on the island of Kribiti where he lives and which is his home. If sea-levels rise by one metre it will be impossible for people to go on living on the island.

Fr Denis Edwards presented a wonderful paper entitled 'Celebrating the Eucharist in a Time of Global Climate Change'. Fr Edwards argued that responding to climate change must be central to our life of faith. He then went on to discuss what global warming might mean for people who gather each Sunday in the name of Jesus to listen to the World of God and break and share bread together. He built a theology of the Eucharist which highlighted the fact that every creature is a living memory of God. Fr Edwards is aware that we come to the Eucharist in a world of broken human realities and ecological destruction. Orthodox theologians see the Eucharist as lifting up to God everything in our world, including its pain and brokenness. The Holy Spirit is invoked to transform the gifts of creation and the community of the faithful into the Body of Christ. Addressing the ecological crisis will require deep commitment and faith. That is why a culture of sharing, built up though the living ethos of a Christian community that is centred on the Eucharist, is the most powerful long-term resource for ecological commitment.[34]

---

34. Denis Edwards, 'Celebrating Eucharist in a Time of Global Climate Change', 2005, www.catholicearthcareoz.com

Another important ecumenical pastoral initiative in Australia is the 'Season of Creation' liturgy which has been developed by the Lutheran theologian and author Normal Habel. He believes that it is essential to bring the message of creation right into the heart of the liturgical cycle of the churches. So he is proposing to add a new Season of Creation to the traditional Advent, Christmas, Lenten and Easter Seasons. This season would fall each year on the four or five Sundays before the Feast of St Francis of Assissi on 4 October. Francis was designated the patron saint of ecology by the late John Paul II in 1979. Every church in the East and West recognises the life and testimony of Francis of Assissi. A Charter for the Season of Creation would include 7 elements:

• Celebrate the earth as a sacred planet filled with God's vibrant presence
• Unite with all creation in praising the God of creation.
• Confess our sins against creation and empathise with a groaning creation.
• Embrace creation as our extended family.
• Proclaim the good news that the risen Jesus is the cosmic Christ who fills and renews all creation.
• Gather all to the Eucharist to receive the healing power of Christ that extends to all creation.
• Go forth on a mission to be partners with Christ in healing all creation.

The calendar for the Season of Creation follows a three year cycle. Year A (2005) is entitled The Spirit in Creation. The first Sunday is Forest Sunday; the second Sunday is Land Sunday; the third Sunday is Outback/Wilderness Sunday and the fourth is River Sunday and the fifth is Planet Sunday. Year B is called the Word in Creation. It has the following themes for four Sundays: Humanity Sunday, Sky Sunday Mountain Sunday and the Blessing of the Animals Sunday. Themes for the C cycle are Ocean Sunday, Fauna Sunday, Storm Sunday and Cosmos Sunday. The idea behind having such liturgies emerged in Australia. They have now been adapted for the US and could

easily be adapted by a liturgy group in a parish for an Irish con-
gregation. There are excellent biblical, musical and IT resources
available on the website www.seasonofcreation.com

*New Zealand Bishops on the Environment*
On September 10, 2006 the New Zealand Bishops issued a pastoral letter entitled 'Our World is Facing an Ecological Crisis'.
They began by quoting from the homily which Pope Benedict
XVI gave at his installation Mass in 2005. 'The external deserts in
the world are growing, because the internal deserts have become so vast. Therefore the earth's treasures no longer serve to
build God's garden for all to live in, but they have been made to
serve the powers of exploitation and destruction.'

The Bishops went on to ask: What does the commandment
'Thou shall not kill' mean when 20% of the world's population
consumes resources at a rate that robs poorer nations and future
generations of what they need to survive?

What does it mean to respect life when 30,000 people die
each day from poverty? What does it mean to be stewards of the
earth when up to half of all living species are expected to become extinct in the next 200 years?

Science and technology have brought many blessings to
human existence. Over the last 50 years those blessings have included a greater capacity to meet basic human needs. But the
benefits of these advances have been spread unjustly, often with
an adverse effect upon the world's most vulnerable populations.
The existence of extreme poverty and environmental destruction in our world are not natural forces, nor acts of God, but result from human behaviour. That behaviour is driven by values,
priorities and decisions which do not see human life as a para-
mount concern.

Our world is facing an ecological crisis, which could equally
be called an economic crisis, or a poverty crisis. Its public face is
the suffering of the poor and the degradation of our environment, at a time when accumulation of wealth and material
goods has never occupied our attention more. That is why we
see it primarily as a spiritual or moral crisis.

Climate scientists warn us that the decisions of this generation over the next 20 years will have an impact upon the future of humanity. For the peoples of the Pacific, climate change is already among the most urgent threats facing them. Rising temperatures and sea levels, and the greater intensity of storms and natural disasters, are already affecting the food and water supply for people on low-lying islands in different parts of the Pacific.

Long before these islands disappear into the sea, life on many Pacific islands will become untenable. It is predicted that in the Pacific alone, there may be a million environmental refugees before the end of this century.

As in other parts of the world, those most suffering the consequences of climate change are those who have played the least part in contributing to it. People we may never meet, as well as those who are not yet born, will benefit or suffer as a result of the decisions we make and take in New Zealand and in the rest of the developed world. As Benedict said in his inaugural homily: 'The external deserts are growing, because the internal deserts have become so vast.'

Protecting the environment involves moderating our desires to consume and own more, which creates lifestyles that bring death to millions of other people. Consumerism, global environmental change and suffering in the developing world are inextricably linked.

At the personal level the suffering of others and the damage to our planet demand that we look closely at our own lifestyles. Individual acts of selfishness can create a society characterised by a desire for short term gain and immediate gratification over longer term needs and a wider view.

In response, both individual and collective acts of selflessness are needed – of self-sacrifice for the greater good, of self denial in the midst of convenient choices, of choosing simpler lifestyles in the midst of a consumer society. This does not mean abandoning the scientific and technological advances which have given us such great benefits. It means using them wisely, and in a thoughtful manner which reflects true solidarity with all the people of the earth.

Ultimately, this is a global problem requiring real global solutions. But individual Catholics, parishes, Catholic schools, religious communities and church organisations can play a big part by making different choices, such as using less energy or buying locally made goods which require less transportation. The world needs to reduce its carbon output by 80%, and some New Zealand households could achieve that overnight by simply changing the kind of car they drive. Avoiding water waste and excess packaging are two simple steps which can be acted upon by individuals and households. But vulnerable members of our own society – such as the elderly – have suffered previously during power crises by going without necessities such as warmth and light, and we have to work to ensure that the costs of any changes to our lifestyles are borne by those who can best afford them.

Our faith and our religious tradition have much to offer the world at this time, including the importance of simplicity, and of learning to give up some things that we want, so others may have what they need. Our understanding that we are stewards of God's creation, our solidarity with the poor, and our respect for the common good make the issue of environmental justice the responsibility of every person.[35]

*British Churches' Response to Environmental Degradation*
Unfortunately, nothing as thorough or creative with regard to environmental degradation has happened in either the church in Ireland or in Britain. As a preparation for the UN 2002 Conference on Environment and Development in Johannesburg the Catholic Bishops' Conference of England and Wales issued a pastoral letter entitled *The Call of Creation*. Obviously the person who drafted this document did not have access to the superior resources that Catholic EarthCare Australia had access to. There

---

35. New Zealand Bishops on the Environment. www.zenit.org. Sept 10. 2006. Down loaded on 23.10.06

is a small section on the global warming but, unfortunately, it failed to address what the British government is doing about this major problem.

There is one positive climate change initiiative in the context of Britain and Ireland called 'Operation Noah'. This is an ecumenical initiative undertaken by a group called Churches Together in Britain and Ireland and is an umbrella body for all the major Christian Churches in Britain and Ireland. Operation Noah is designed to curb human-induced climate change. It was launched in October 2004 in Coventry and over 200 activists attended the conference that launched the campaign. They were invited to sign a covenant promising to reduce their own greenhouse gas emissions. They were also encouraged to put pressure on the British government and world leaders to so likewise. Churches were lobbied to source their electricity from renewable suppliers. The co-ordinator of Operation Noah is Paul Bodenham. He feels that the concept of covenant has deep roots in the Judeo-Christian tradition and Operation Noah is inviting Christians to make a covenant, which will help some of the most vulnerable people and ecosystems on the planet.

This theme also emerged in a letter from Ms Grace Akumu, who is the co-ordinator of Climate Network Africa. According to her, 'Africa's hopes and aspirations are being dashed by the blind pursuit of economic development in the industrialised countries.' The delegates from all over Britain gave a standing ovation to Ed Beale when he entered the hall. Ed is a 27 year old Baptist who walked the length of Britain from John O'Groats to Lands End to raise awareness about 'Operation Noah' and climate change in the various churches. The campaign is a response to God's call to humans in Genesis to respect and protect creation. It takes its inspiration from the Noah Story in the Book of Genesis. Noah was directed by God to protect not only his own family but the rest of creation. He was told to take two of each animal so that they would be saved from extinction. (Gen 6: 17-22).

The Rainbow Covenant included all creation. The campaign

also taps into the prophetic tradition in the Hebrew Scriptures. Prophets appeared when Israel had turned away from God or were in denial about some important value. Operation Noah believes that there is a collective denial around global warming. It is the role of the prophetic ministry to challenge this complacency by pointing out what the consequence of doing nothing will be for the next generation. The Campaign sees itself in continuity with Moses who challenged the people of Israel before entering the Promised Land. At the end of the book of Deuteronomy he says: 'I set before you life or death, blessing or curse. Choose life, then, so that you and your descendants may live' (Deut 30:19b-20a). This is a perfect slogan for the campaign because it recognises that the longer the international community prevaricates on this crucial issue the less time there will be for effective solutions and the greater the pain and disruption will be for future generations of all life. Thankfully some Catholics in Britain are involved with global warming issues with Operation Noah but a lot more support from Catholic Church leaders is required if it is going to become an issue in Catholic parishes.

There are other green shoots of hope. The theme of the National Justice and Peace Network's Conference in Derbyshire in 2005 was 'We are Stewards of Creation'. More than 300 justice and peace activists attended and embraced the message enthusiastically; but this message needs to seep out into the deepest recesses of parish life and grasp the imagination of the bishops. The latter still have the power to allocate the resources which will be necessary to develop sustainable policies and programmes. The bishops will need to listen to people with expertise in a wide range of environmental disciplines – ethics, theology, economics, transport, energy, communications and food policies, to mention just a few. But this is how our community of church should operate.

The Anglican Church in Britain is beginning to take climate change very seriously. In 2005, the General Synod debated *Sharing God's Planet*, a Report from the Church's Mission and Public Affairs Council. The report called for a measured reduction in energy consumption in the Church of England before 2008. In May 2006, the Archbishop of Canterbury, Rowan Williams spoke at the Tynndall Centre For Climate Change and said that the Church of England was about to launch a 'shrinking footprint' exercise. This involves getting every building and diocesan office to measure its current energy consumption and then to set targets to reduce their greenhouse gas emissions.[36]

To coincide with World Environment Day, 5 June 2006, all the dioceses in England received an Audit Pack to undertake the required assessment of current levels and types of energy consumption in church buildings in every parish. Church people from the locality were invited to promote discussion on these issues. The audit resources, as far as possible, were distributed electronically to keep paper consumption to a minimum. The Bishop of London, Dr Richard Chartres headed up the church's 'Shrinking the Footprint Campaign'. More information is available on www.shrinkinigthefootprint.anglican.org>

*Churches in Ireland Silent on Ecological Destruction*
The Irish environment has seen many, mostly deleterious changes, since the 1960s.For example, more than 180 golf courses have been built in every habitat in Ireland from parklands to sand dunes. Many were built without requiring planning permission, yet all of them altered the environment in a significant, adverse ways. Emissions from industry, run-offs from agricultural lands and poor sanitation facilities have contributed to the deterioration of water quality, especially our ground water. However, it is important to acknowledge that there are not as many fish kills at the present time as there were in the 1980s. Farmers are much more vigilant and have proper storage facilities for their silage effluent. However Environmental Protection Agency (EPA) reports every year draw attention to the fact that many of the rural water schemes are contaminated.

Farming practices, especially the cultivation of rye grass,

---

36.'Zeal of approval', *The Guardian, Society/Guardian/Environment,* 17 May 2006, page 8.

puts pressure on many plant and animal species in Ireland. Mountains have been overgrazed. There is a dire need to protect biodiversity in Ireland at the moment. Road building projects are gobbling up 25,000 hectares of prime land, though peak-oil and climate change might make these roads useless for our transport needs in 20 or 30 years' time. Waste disposal is also a major issue, with many communities facing the possibility of living in the vicinity of domestic and toxic waste incinerators. Finally, as I have said before, Ireland is now 23% above the emissions quota which was allotted to it in the Kyoto Protocol.

The response from the Irish churches to all of these appalling scenarios has been almost total silence. The Archbishop of Cashel and Emly, Dr Dermot Clifford did publish a pastoral letter on water entitled *The Whole of Creation is Groaning*, and Bishop Murphy mentioned the environment in his pastoral letter for the millennium. In a Pastoral Letter entitled, *Towards the Global Common Good*, in 2005 the Irish Catholic bishops wrote: 'On the national level much needs to be done to cut Ireland's greenhouse gas emissions. As a nation we are legally bound to fulfill our obligations under the Kyoto Protocol which came into force in February 2005. According to the most recent review of the government's National Climate Change Strategy projections, Ireland will not reach its targets set under the Kyoto Protocol. It is a moral imperative, therefore, that the measures set out in the National Climate Change Strategy in 2000 are implemented with greater speed. All of us have a part to play: homes, schools, parishes, businesses and government. All of us can review our own practices and establish our own challenging targets to ensure that we meet our moral obligations to care for creation as God intended and to create a sustainable environment.'[37]

This letter is not well known. We need more education and effective guidance from the leadership of the churches.

---

37. *Towards the Global Common Good*, Pastoral Letter on International Development from the Irish Bishops' Conference, 2005, Veritas, Dublin, page 10.

It is a shame that the Irish churches cannot come together and work to protect the Irish environment by promoting a low-carbon lifestyle which would keep the rise in global temperature as low as possible. What a testimony it would be to the relevance and influence of religion, if the churches in Ireland and members of other religious faiths, such as Islam, Buddhism and Hinduism could all work closely together to tackle environmental problems and especially global warming. A world of searing heat will not distinguish between Hindu, Buddhist, Church of Ireland, Presbyterians or Catholics. It will have the same destructive impact on everyone. Protecting our land, rivers and climate is one area where the churches could unite.

One of the better internet sites for churches and the environment is the EcoCongregation website at www.ecocongregation.org> It was set up through a partnership arrangement between the churches and the government in Britain. It is funded by the environmental charity ENCAMS (which runs the Keep Britain Tidy Campaign and the Going Green brand) and the Environmental Issues Network of Churches Together in Britain and Ireland.

A kit can be downloaded from the website which will enable one to conduct an environmental check-up/audit of a parish. The survey identifies the existing good practice if any and points out where the parish can prioritise areas for eco-development. It provides resources for worship, study and many aspects of parish life. It gives tips on how to start to move along the road to become an eco-congregation. There are 12 Modules with titles such as 'Creation and Christianity'. These modules offer perspectives for theological discussion groups and sermons. Module 10, 'Green Choices' offers information and suggestions on how to develop a green lifestyle and the resources that are necessary to achieve that goal.

At the bottom of the website there is a link to eco-congregation in Ireland. However when I accessed the site it carried the following message:

We hope you and your church will find this site a practical

help in making the link between the environment and your faith. You will find that many of the stories and experiences relate to English and Scottish churches but as Irish churches enroll in the programme, we will be augmenting and replacing them with our own experiences. We welcome feedback, so please contact us with suggestions, comments and inevitable corrections. We hope that you find this site useful and informative and we wish you every success in your environmental adventure!

The date on the site was 2005 and nothing has been added since. It truly reflects the huge lack of awareness of the environment in all Irish churches. That needs to change radically and quickly.

One bright light on the Irish ecclesiastical scene is Cardinal Cahal B. Daly, Emeritus Catholic Archbishop of Armagh. One can only have the highest regard for the energy, courage and pastoral sensitivity of this man. In his retirement he set about understanding the magnitude of the environmental issue. He is now probably the best informed senior church leader in Ireland on the environment. In 2004, he wrote an excellent book on ecology, social justice and religion entitled *The Minding of Planet Earth*. Most of the data for his ecological reflections come from *Global 2000 Report to the President*. This was a research programme initiated by President Jimmy Carter in 1977. The data on global warming is very accurate. It states that 'atmospheric concentration of carbon dioxide will be nearly one-third higher than pre-industrial levels'.[38]

Cardinal Daly realises the magnitude of the ecological crisis and the urgency with which it must be faced. A sentence on the back cover states bluntly that these issues must 'be faced with urgency if catastrophes on a cosmic scale are to be averted'. These are very strong words from a man who, given his philosophical training and his years as a pastor in a divided society in Northern Ireland, has always been very careful with what he says and how he says it.

---

38. Cardinal Cahal Daly, *The Minding of Planet Earth*, Veritas, Dublin, 2004, pages 184-5.

Pope Benedict XVI called attention to the ecological side of the Eucharist in his homily on the Feast of Corpus Christi on 15 June 2006. He affirmed that the consecrated host is the 'food of the poor' and 'fruit of the earth and of the labour of mankind'. He added that 'the bread is not simply our own product, something made by us: it is a fruit of the earth, and hence a gift. It requires the synergy of the forces of the earth and of the gift of heaven: sun and rain.' He went on to say that: 'At a time in which we hear of desertification, and there is ever more talk of the danger of men and beasts dying of thirst in those regions without water, at such a time we gain a renewed awareness of the greatness of the gift of water, and how incapable we are of producing it alone. Then, looking closer at this little piece of Host, this bread of the poor appears as a synthesis of creation.' He linked in a beautiful way Creation and Jesus: 'When, in adoration, we contemplate the consecrated Host, the mark of creation is speaking to us. Then we discover the greatness of this gift, but we also discover the past, the cross of Jesus and his resurrection.'[39] These profound understandings of the Eucharist provide the well-spring of energy to engage with global warming and other ecological challenges.

*Practical Ways to Address Climate Change*

All the churches should encourage Christians to adopt a more energy friendly lifestyle, especially in their use of fossil fuel. In an Irish and British context, these are some easy steps which everyone can use to lessen our fossil fuel dependency in the house:

1  Turn down the thermostat in your home by 1 degree celsius. This can save over 10% on your fuel bill and also pump less carbon dioxide into the atmosphere. If you feel a little cold then wear extra clothes.

2  Very often when we turn on the hot tap scalding water flows

---

39. Vatican Information Service, *The Consecrated Host Truly Is the Bread of Heaven*, Sermon of Pope Benedict XVI on the Feast of Corpus Christi at the Basilica of St John Lateran on June 15, 2006.

within 30 seconds. Many people will find that a setting of around 60 degrees celsius will be quite adequate for their needs. In your bathroom why not install a spray tap? This delivers as little as a cup of water for every half bucket from an ordinary tap.

3   In the kitchen. When buying electrical appliances like fridges, freezers, dishwasher or ovens always look at their energy efficiency. Remember that pressure cookers and microwave ovens use less energy than conventional ones.

4   Make sure that the cylinder in your hot press is lagged to minimise the loss of heat.

5   Good insulation reduces both the heating bill and carbon dioxide. Double-glazing is an ideal way to reduce heat loss. While the initial capital costs are high, the return in terms of reduced heating bills is significant. In addition, always close the curtains in your house when the heating system is on. It is important to insulate your roof properly. Hot air rises and a considerable amount can escape through the roof if it is not properly insulated.

6   Ensure that your attic is well insulated. If the insulation in your attic is less than 250mm you are advised to add further layers. There is a variety of suitable material, from sheep's wool to polystyrene, cellulose fibre and multilayered foil.

7   Avoid using electric lights when there is a good source of natural light. Use energy saving bulbs where possible. These bulbs use only one quarter of the energy used by standard bulbs. At present energy saving bulbs are more expensive than conventional ones but the reduced running costs will mean that it will be possible to recoup your initial outlay in a short period. Remember that televisions and computers use almost as much energy in their standby mode as when they are fully functioning. All lights on appliances should be turned off when not in use.

8   When you are making tea or coffee boil only as much water as is necessary.

9   Christian Ecology Link, which is composed of Christians

from many churches, is an invaluable resource in developing a Christian ecological consciousness. Its website is well worth visiting at www.christian-ecology.org.uk> Its home-page is well organised and leads one directly to campaigns which are presently running or supporting initiatives like 'Operation Noah'. There is a section on current ecological problems which is very helpful. A section on practical ideas gives many tips for living in a more ecological friendly way. There is also a diary which is mainly related to ecological events happening in Britain. There is a section of suitable prayers and also links to other comparable sites. This excel-lent site is edited by volunteers.

By placing global warming on the top of their agenda, the Christian churches would first of all be giving much needed leadership in facing up to one of the most crucial issues of our time. If the teaching and pastoral priorities of the churches were more focused on these issues, the churches would be demon-strating that they take seriously God's love for our world (John 3:16-17). They would also be fulfilling their prophetic role in challenging the forces that are destroying the planet and, by doing this, they would be promoting a more sustainable way of living. This would attract people who are deeply concerned about global warming. Like Attenborough, anyone who looks in the eyes of children must be concerned by the fact that their own behaviour is causing significant changes which are now trigger-ing global warming. Many of those people would be delighted if the churches, particularly the Catholic Church, could shake it-self out of it current lethargy on environmental issues and throw its full weight behind a campaign like 'Operation Noah'.

*Time to change – Now*
There is no time to lose. There is a consensus building in the sci-entific world that we have, at the most, twenty years to take de-cisive action on climate change, othervise we will have passed irreversible 'tipping points'. If we continue with a business-as-usual approach in relation to fossil fuel, we will set in train plan-

etary changes, like the melting of the Greenland ice sheet and the break-up of large areas of the Antartic ice sheet, which will make this world an inhospitable place.

For the past few centuries, the myth of progress encouraged each succeeding generation of humans to believe that they would enjoy a better standard of living than the previous generation. If carbon levels rise to 450 parts per million, then a constant feedback process will ensure that it will make the earth a less hospitable place for each succeeding generation of humans and other creatures. In terms of sea levels rising, for example, each succeeding generation will know that climate conditions will be worse for the next generation until thermal expansion has worked its way slowly through the oceans. But there will be an inevitability about the deterioration that will make life difficult for humans to endure. Future generations will not forgive the two generations at the end of the 20th century and beginning of the 21st century who knew what they were doing but continued to pollute the atmosphere.

It is important that the changes begin now. We are certainly living in a time of unprecedented crisis for the natural world. From a Christian theological perspective, we are living in a *kairos* moment. It demands concrete choices for individuals and institutions to help bring about this new age. We need inspired political leadership because, no matter what individuals do to address global warming, if the political and economic community does not come on board, little will be achieved. We need politicians like Al Gore, former Vice-President of the US, who have the courage to explain to the public what is at stake in the whole area of global warming and who will lead people to make the kind of changes which will be necessary. Carbon taxes are merely the beginning of a comprehensive approach that lessens our use of fossil fuel and develops a range of alternative energy sources.

The church, as a 'sign raised up among the nations', should be in the forefront of these efforts because what is at stake are ultimately ethical and religious issues. Those in positions of authority in the churches must give much more effective leadership than they have to date. A wider ecological pastoral approach must be at the centre of ministry in the churches. On the practical level, many organisations – the *World Wide Fund, Green Peace, Green Parties*, the *UN, Friends of the Earth, Green Consumer Organisations* – are helping us to understand the issues and making available the possibility of concrete choices. On a religious level, we should try to evolve a theology, spirituality and a missiology which is sensitive to the presence of God in the natural world. Rituals that celebrate God's presence are vitally important in order to reconnect us in an integral way with the natural world. We must develop these for our homes, schools, and Christian communities. This will call forth creativities which at present lie dormant in the community of the church. In the sacraments we use symbols from the natural world – water, oil, wine, light, darkness – but they are often used in an anaemic way that alienates us rather than connects us with the natural world.

Let me finish on a positive note. On the Feast of Pentecost we call on the Holy Spirit: 'Come, O Holy Spirit, fill the hearts of your faithful and enkindle in them the fire of your love. Send forth your spirit and they shall be created and you will renew the face of the earth.' This is our challenge and this is our prayer. We know that the God who created this beautiful world mourns the destruction which is taking place in our times, and that he is calling on all of us to dedicate ourselves to healing and caring for the earth. The worldwide growth of the ecological movement, and the move to incorporate this into the missionary dimension of the church, is a sign, to use the words of the poet Gerald Manley Hopkins:

That the Holy Ghost over the bent
World broods with warm breast and ah!
bright wings.

# Websites on Climate Change

Christian-Ecology link: www.christian-ecology.org.uk
Eco-congregation: www.ecocongregation.org
    www.emagazine.com
Friends of the Earth (FOE): www.foe.co.uk
Friends of the Earth (Ireland): www.foe.ie
Gore, Al, *An Inconvenient Truth*: www.climatecrisis.net
International Panel on Climate Change: www.ipcc.ch
Oxford Declaration on Climate Change:
    www.climateforum2002.org
Nuclear Spin: www.nuclearspin.org/
Peak-Oil: www.peakoil.com
UN Environment Programme: www.climateimc.org
Union of Concerned Scientists:
    www.ucsusa.org/.../global-warming-fag.html

# Bibliography

Anil Makhandya and Kirsten, 2002, *Climate Change and Sustainable Development*, Earthscan, London.

A. Barrie Pittock, 2005, *Turning up the Heat*, Earthscan, London.

Amory B. Lovings, 1979, *Soft Energy Paths*, Harper and Row, New York.

Cardinal Cahal Daly, 2004, *The Minding of Planet Earth*, Veritas, Dublin.

*Compendium of the Social Doctrine of the Church*, 2004, Veritas, Dublin.

David Hollenback, SJ, 2002, *The Common Good and Christian Ethics*, Cambridge University Press, Washington DC.

Fred Pearce, 2005, *The Last Generation – How Nature Will Take Her Revenge for Climate Change*, Eden Project Books.

*Energy in Ireland, 1990-2004, Trends, issues, forecasts and indicators*, Sustainable Energy Ireland.

Godfrey Boyle (ed) 2004, *Renewable Energy: Power for a Sustainable Future*, Oxford University Press with the Open University.

James Lovelock, 2006, *The Revenge of Gaia*, Penguin, London.

Jared Diamond, 2005, *Collapse: How Societies Choose to Fail or Survive*, Allen Lane, an imprint of Penguin Books, London.

Jeremy Leggett, 1990, *Global Warming: The Greenpeace Report*, Oxford University Press, Oxford.

John Houghton, 2004, *Global Warming*, Cambridge University Press, Cambridge.

John Sweeney, et al, 2004, *Climate Change: Scenario and Impacts for Ireland*, Environmental Protection Agency (EPA), PO Box 3000, Johnstown Castle, Co Wexford, Ireland.

Kenneth S. Deffeyes, 2005, *Beyond Oil: The View from Hubbert's Peak,* Hill and Wang, a division of Farrar, Straus and Giroux, New York.

Martin Rees, 2003, *Our Final Century: Will The Human Race Survive he Twenty-First Century?* William Heinemann, London.

*Our Common Future*, The World Commission on Environment and Development, 1987, Oxford University Press.

Seán McDonagh,1999, *Greening the Christian Millennium*, Dominican Publications, Dublin.

*Sign of Peril, Test of Faith, Accelerated Climate Change*, 1994, World
    Council of Churches, 150, route de Ferney, PO Box 2100, 1211
    Geneva 2, Switzerland.

Tim Flannery, 2005, *The Weather Makers: History and Future Impact of
    Climate Change*, Allen Lane, (Penguin), London.

Richard Douthwaite (ed), 2003, *Before the Wells Run Dry: Ireland's
    Transition to Renewable Energy*, Lilliput Press, 159 Lower Rathmines
    Road, Dublin 6.

*The Future of Renewable Energy 2*, EURED Agency 2002, James and James
    (Science Publishers) 35-37, William Road, London, NW1 3ER.

G. B. Marini-Bettólo 1989, *Study Week on A MODERN APPROACH TO
    THE PROTECTION OF THE ENVIRONMENT*, Pontifical Academy
    of the Sciences, Vatican City, Rome.

# Index